The
Revolutionary War

VOLUME 7

The Revolutionary War

VOLUME 7

War of Attrition

James R. Arnold & Roberta Wiener

GROLIER

An imprint of

SCHOLASTIC

Scholastic Library Publishing

www.scholastic.com/librarypublishing

First published 2001 by Grolier
An imprint of Scholastic Library Publishing
Old Sherman Turnpike
Danbury, Connecticut 06816

For information address the publisher:
Scholastic Library Publishing, Old Sherman Turnpike,
Danbury, Connecticut 06816

Reprinted in 2006

Library of Congress Cataloging-in-Publication Data

The Revolutionary War.
     p. cm.
   Contents: v. 1. The road to rebellion—v. 2. The shot heard around
the world—v. 3. Taking up arms—v. 4. The spirit of 1776—v. 5.
1777: A year of decision—v. 6. The road to Valley Forge—v. 7. War of
attrition—v. 8. The American cause in peril—v. 9. The turn of the tide
—v. 10. An independent nation.
   Includes bibliographical references and indexes.
     ISBN 0-7172-5553-0 (set)—ISBN 0-7172-5554-9 (v. 1)—
ISBN 0-7172-5555-7 (v. 2)—ISBN 0-7172-5556-5 (v. 3)—
ISBN 0-7172-5557-3 (v. 4)—ISBN 0-7172-5558-1 (v. 5)—
ISBN 0-7172-5559-X (v. 6)—ISBN 0-7172-5560-3 (v. 7)—
ISBN 0-7172-5561-1 (v. 8)—ISBN 0-7172-5562-X (v. 9)—
ISBN 0-7172-5563-8 (v. 10)
     1. United States—History—Revolution, 1775–1783—Juvenile
literature. [1. united States—History—Revolution. 1775–1783.]
     I. Grolier Incorporated.
E208 .R.47   2002   8970
973.3—dc21   2001018998

Printed and bound in Singapore

CONTENTS

CHAPTER ONE

THE WAR AT SEA 6

CHAPTER TWO

THE AMAZING JOHN PAUL JONES 20

CHAPTER THREE

THE IMPACT OF THE FRENCH 32

CHAPTER FOUR

THE BRITISH EVACUATE PHILADELPHIA 40

CHAPTER FIVE

THE BATTLE OF MONMOUTH 49

CHAPTER SIX

THE BRITISH TURN SOUTH 58

CHRONOLOGY 69

GLOSSARY 70

FURTHER RESOURCES 71

SET INDEX 72

ACKNOWLEDGMENTS 80

CHAPTER ONE

The War at Sea

British and American warships engage off Cape Sable, Newfoundland on July 7, 1777.

When the Revolutionary War began, the British navy (called the Royal Navy) was in very bad condition. The British government had neglected the Royal Navy in order to save money. Many of its ships were unseaworthy, meaning they could not go to sea for very long before they had to return for repairs. The special kind of lumber needed to build new ships was in short supply.

A politician named Lord John Sandwich headed the Admiralty (the organization that ran the navy). He was not very good at his job. Sandwich allowed a great deal of corruption. In the words of one historian, important positions of leadership "were bought, stores [naval supplies] were stolen and, worst of all, ships, unseaworthy and inadequately equipped, were sent to fight the battles of their country." Neither were the navy's officers and men as skilled as those of the past.

Yet the Royal Navy was still the most powerful navy in the world. It had the most ships. In 1775 the Royal Navy had 131 ships of the line (the battleships of the **Age of Sail**) and 139 other types of warships. Most important, the Royal Navy had a tremendous amount of experience and what is called a tradition of victory. British seamen knew that in the past the Royal Navy had defeated its enemies. The combination of experience and tradition gave them confidence that they could win again.

At the time of the battles of Lexington and Concord (see Volume 2) a small naval force of only 30 British ships was on the North American coast. Thirty ships were enough for peacetime purposes but far too few to fight a war against the thirteen rebellious colonies. British naval officials soon decided to expand the Royal Navy. By the end of 1776, 74 ships were assigned to North America. That still was not enough to do all of the things that needed doing.

The Royal Navy escorted, or guarded, the ships that brought soldiers and supplies from Europe to North

Age of Sail: the period of history before engines were invented, when ships used sails to move across the water

The Royal Navy

The British government prepared for another war with France even before France allied with the American rebels. The Royal Navy began a rapid expansion as early as 1776. It needed ships and sailors. A new ship of the line took up to six years to build. To avoid delay, the navy kept a reserve of ships in storage. The navy began preparing the reserve ships in order to be ready to fight the French. At the same time, the ships already in service needed a great deal of work to keep them at sea.

Keeping the Royal Navy at sea was an enormous job. Building and repair of warships took place at six main Royal Dockyards in England. The dockyards employed more than 10,000 workers. Many of them were skilled craftsmen such as carpenters, ropemakers, sailmakers, and metalworkers. The Royal Dockyards formed Britain's, and probably the world's, largest industrial complex. By the end of the Revolutionary War the dockyards were responsible for over 600 warships, the largest single naval force the world had yet seen.

Service in the Royal Navy was so miserable that there were never enough volunteers to crew the ships. Yet a large warship required a

Above: A gun deck on a ship of the line. During a battle the deck filled with dense smoke, and the noise of the cannons being fired caused men to lose their hearing.

Below: The most powerful ships of the line had three decks, one on top of the other, with each deck carrying a line of cannons.

crew that numbered hundreds of men. A 74-gun ship of the line, the most common type of British battleship, needed a crew of about 650 men. To get enough sailors, captains in the Royal Navy had the power to take men and force them to serve aboard their ships. This was called the press. Captains sent armed sailors, called press gangs, to stop British merchant ships and take, or press, sailors from the merchant ships. They also sent the press gangs to seize men who lived along the coast, especially men who lived in seaports.

The press gangs searched for experienced sailors, but able-bodied men of all sorts were useful. A sailing ship needed many men to do hard labor such as raising the anchor and hauling on the ropes to set a sail. Pressed men who had no naval experience or skill could learn to do such jobs. If the men seemed unwilling or worked too slowly, they were beaten or flogged (whipped). Discipline was so severe in the Royal Navy that thousands of men tried to desert. If a deserter was caught, he faced terrible punishment, often death. For

many men life aboard a warship was like living in a floating jail. A famous British writer asked, "I wonder why men go to sea while there are jails on shore?" The answer was that they had no choice.

About half of a typical warship's crew were pressed men, most of whom were experienced sailors. About fifteen percent were volunteers, and another fifteen percent were criminals who were given the choice of jail or service aboard a ship. About twelve percent were foreigners, mostly men who had been unlucky to have been stranded in British ports and then caught by a press gang. Even young boys could do useful chores on a ship, so charitable groups sent thousands of orphans, strays, and delinquents to the Royal Navy.

During the course of the Revolutionary War the Royal Navy raised 171,000 men. Only 1,240 died in battle. Disease killed 18,500, and another 42,000 deserted.

Left: Warships needed large crews with hundreds of sailors both to work the cannons and to work the sails.

America. That duty alone was a huge task. By the summer of 1776 almost 500 British transport ships (ships that transport men, horses, and supplies) were sailing back and forth across the Atlantic. In order to make the job of protecting the transports easier, the Admiralty organized the transports into convoys, or

The American warship *Andrea Doria* receives a salute from the Dutch colony of St. Eustatius on November 16, 1776. This was the first time a foreign power saluted an American warship.

groups of ships. Escorting the convoys across the Atlantic was one of the navy's most important duties.

In North American waters the Royal Navy also had to support the army. That meant transporting the army wherever it needed to go in North America, keeping it supplied once it got there, and using the guns of the warships to bombard rebel targets on land. The duty of supporting the army took most of the Royal Navy's strength in North America. In 1776, 54 out of the 74 warships were helping the army. The remaining 20 were not nearly enough to accomplish the other Royal Navy assignment, the blockade of the American coast.

The thirteen rebellious colonies manufactured very few of the things the rebels needed to fight the war. Muskets, cannons, medicine, tents, blankets, uniforms, and especially gunpowder had to come from Europe on board ships. The Royal Navy tried to intercept these ships. Although the Royal Navy captured many ships carrying war supplies, enough ships passed through the British blockade to supply the rebel army so it could keep fighting.

British military **strategy** during 1776–77 depended on the Royal Navy controlling the waters off the North American coast. That control allowed the Royal Navy to evacuate Boston in March 1776 (see Volume 3) and to land Howe's army on Staten Island for the New York Campaign (see Volume 4) later in the year. Control of the waters off the American coast let the British freely choose which places to attack because the Americans did not have a navy strong enough to interfere.

The Continental Navy

During the Siege of Boston (April 1775 to March 1776; see Volume 3) George Washington organized a small fleet of seven ships to attack British supply ships. The

strategy: the overall plan for a battle or campaign

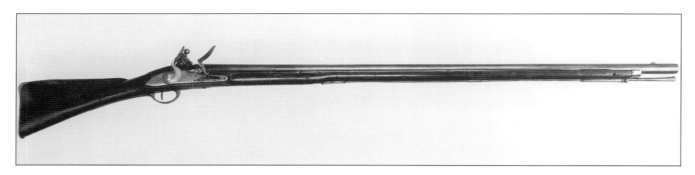

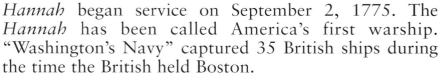

Left: American gunsmiths copied British models to manufacture muskets. Because America had very little manufacturing, the army relied on French imports.

Below Right: Congress appointed Esek Hopkins as the first commander of the Continental Navy.

Two small Continental Navy warships, the 8-gun schooner *Fly* and the 4-gun sloop *Mosquito*

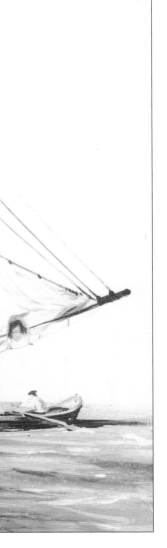

Hannah began service on September 2, 1775. The *Hannah* has been called America's first warship. "Washington's Navy" captured 35 British ships during the time the British held Boston.

On October 19, 1775, Congressman John Adams wrote a letter to James Warren asking, "What think you of an American fleet?" Adams knew that an American fleet could not fight the British on equal terms. However, Adams thought that an American navy could help the rebel cause. New England had many experienced merchants and sailors. New England delegates liked Adams' idea. They persuaded Congress to buy four small ships. Workers added cannons and made other changes so the ships could attack British

Main Picture: Compared to the resources of the Royal Navy, American shipyards were small and primitive.

transports in the Boston area. The *Cabot*, *Andrea Doria*, *Alfred*, and *Columbus* were the first warships of the Continental Navy.

Congress appointed John Adams to head a Naval Committee that made naval strategy. It also created a Marine Corps on November 10, appointed Esek Hopkins as commander-in-chief of the navy, and ordered eight more ships to be bought and converted to warships. In December Congress ordered the building

Above: The offer of food and drink brought Marine recruits to the Old Tun Tavern in Philadelphia.

The Continental Navy's first flag, which was flown while in port, showed a rattlesnake with the inscription "Don't Tread on Me." The yellow flag with the coiled rattlesnake served as Esek Hopkins' command flag.

On March 3, 1776, 270 sailors and Continental Marines landed at New Providence to attack the island of Nassau.

of thirteen frigates, the cruisers of the age of sail. Congress stated that the frigates had to be built by March 1776.

Americans had never built such large warships before. England had special dockyards to build warships. England also had experienced naval architects, skilled craftsmen, and the special materials needed to build warships. American builders had to overcome all sorts of shortages to build their frigates. For example, they had no seasoned wood (timber that has been cut and dried for several years). So, the Americans built their frigates out of freshly cut trees, which shrank and twisted as they dried. Some of the American frigates proved to be poorly built. But some proved to be good warships.

While the American frigates were being built, Congress ordered Esek Hopkins to clear Chesapeake Bay of British ships, drive the British from the Carolina coast, and then attack the British off the Rhode Island coast. That was far too hard an assignment for eight ships with 110 guns. Because the British had sent more ships to the American coast, the eight American ships had to face 78 British ships with more than 2,000 guns. Hopkins managed to raid Nassau, in the Bahamas, in March 1776. There the Marines fought the first battle in Marine Corps history. The rebels captured over 100 artillery pieces and many valuable supplies.

But Hopkins failed to do all that Congress had hoped. In the spring Congress removed Hopkins from his position as the highest ranking Continental Navy officer.

Just like the Continental Army, the Continental Navy had trouble recruiting men. Unlike the Royal Navy, the Continental Navy did not use press gangs. Early in the war many men eagerly volunteered. But as time passed, sailors saw that the Continental Navy had strict discipline and low pay. It became harder and harder to find crews. The lack of crews and a shortage of supplies kept many other Continental ships stuck in harbor.

The Continental Navy needed to gain battle experience in order to fight the British and win. That would take time. Meanwhile, the British defeated, captured, and destroyed many rebel ships. Over the course of the entire war the Continental Navy sent into service a total of 53 ships. Those ships captured 196 British ships.

Privateering

Although the thirteen colonies had never built large warships, the Americans did have a long tradition of using privateers. Privateers were armed ships belonging to private individuals and carrying an official government document that let them attack enemy merchantmen (trading ships) and warships. Private men-of-war, or privateers, needed official government approval because without such approval they were pirates. Crews of captured privateers enjoyed the same legal protection as professional sailors. Captured pirates were hanged.

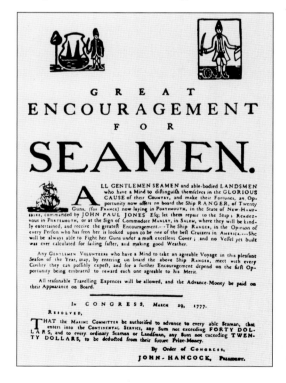

A recruiting poster for the Continental Navy

Landing Soldiers from the Sea

The Royal Navy used some very modern methods for landing soldiers on enemy territory. Good planning and organization were essential. Soldiers and supplies boarded the transports in the order that they would be needed, so that when they got off the transports, they would immediately be ready to fight. Soldiers moved from the transports onto specially built rowboats to land. The rowboats were usually 36 feet long by 10 feet wide. Ten sailors on each side rowed the boats. Two rows of soldiers sat between the rowers.

During the landing of British troops to take Rhode Island in 1776 the landing boats formed into four divisions. The first division carried the soldiers who were to make the first attack—elite light infantry and grenadiers supported by artillery. The second division carried two brigades whose job was to reinforce the attacking soldiers. The third division carried the Hessians, and the fourth carried the cavalry. The landings began at 8 A.M. and were completed by 3 P.M.

Below: The Continental brig USS *Lexington* carried 16 small 4-pounder cannons.

Below Insert: The USS *Surprise* captures a ship just off the British coast in 1778.

People went into privateering to make money. Privateers tried to capture merchantmen, take them into friendly ports, and sell their ships and cargoes. The privateers' owner and crew divided the money. It did no good for a privateer to sink an enemy ship. A privateer also tried to avoid fighting enemy warships. A well-led or lucky privateer could make the owner and crew rich.

In March 1776, three months before the Declaration of Independence, Congress resolved, "That the inhabitants of these Colonies be permitted to fit out armed vessels, to cruise on the enemies of these United Colonies." Congress's resolution began an enormous privateering campaign. The typical privateer carried 20 guns and a crew of about 100 men. No one knows the exact number of rebel privateers that went to sea. Individual states also allowed privateers. Because of its seafaring tradition, Massachusetts was the most active state with probably more than 500 privateers. Estimates of the number of privateers during the whole war vary from about 1,100 to 2,000 ships. Because of the possibility of becoming rich and because life aboard a privateer was much easier than life aboard a Continental Navy warship, most of the best sailors joined privateers. About 11,000 sailors served on privateers during the war.

The privateers were both good and bad for the rebel cause. On the plus side, during the war privateers captured about 600 British ships, including 16 Royal Navy warships. On the minus side it was hard for the Continental Navy to recruit sailors because experienced sailors preferred the privateers. So many men and so much material went into privateering that little was left for the Continental Navy. For that reason the Continental Navy never became an important force during the war. By 1781 the Americans had about 450 privateers and only three Continental Navy ships.

CHAPTER TWO

The Amazing John Paul Jones

Even though the Continental Navy never became a powerful force, some of its ships and some of its leaders won notable fights against the Royal Navy. No one performed better than John Paul Jones. For good reason Jones emerged from the war as the best-remembered American naval officer.

John Paul Jones

John Paul Jones was born in Scotland in 1747. He became an apprentice to a ship owner and at the age of 12 made his first voyage across the Atlantic Ocean to Virginia. He later worked aboard a slave-trading ship and then became a captain of a merchantman. The beginning of the Revolutionary War found him in America living in poverty.

Jones traveled to Philadelphia to help fit out the *Alfred*, the first naval ship bought by Congress. He made friends with two congressmen who used their influence to have Jones appointed as the *Alfred*'s senior first lieutenant (the rank just below captain in the Continental Navy). In 1776 he received his first independent command. He showed so much ability that he was promoted to captain of his own ship. During one of his first cruises as a captain his ship captured 16 British vessels.

Congress sent him to France to take command of the sloop *Ranger*. The *Ranger* had 18 small cannons and a crew of about 140 men. On April 10, 1778, Jones departed France for a raid against Whitehaven, the

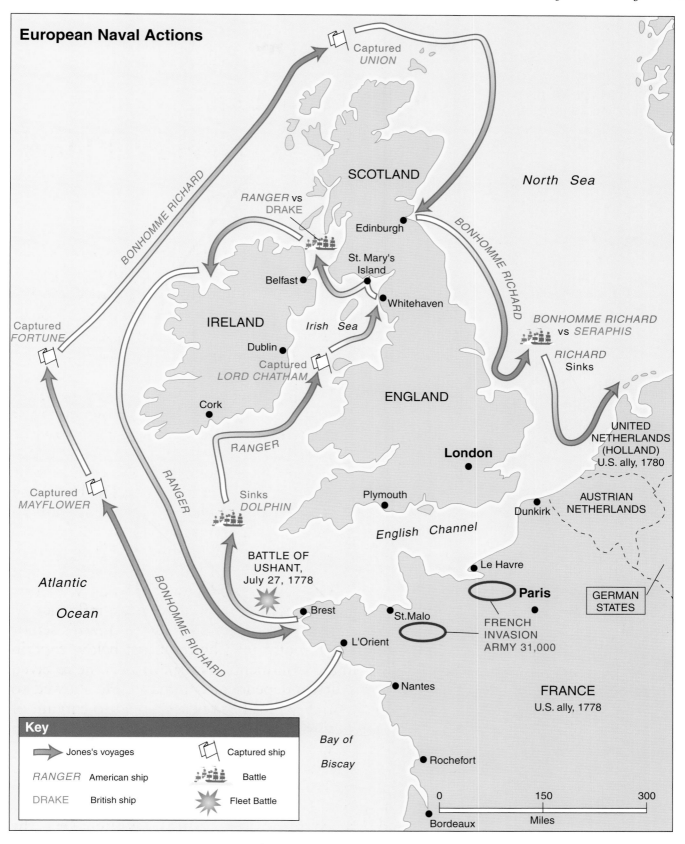

European Naval Actions

Captured
UNION

SCOTLAND

North Sea

RANGER vs
DRAKE

BONHOMME RICHARD

Edinburgh

St. Mary's
Island

BONHOMME RICHARD

Belfast

Whitehaven

BONHOMME RICHARD
vs *SERAPHIS*

Captured
FORTUNE

IRELAND

Irish Sea

RICHARD
Sinks

Dublin

Captured
LORD CHATHAM

ENGLAND

UNITED
NETHERLANDS
(HOLLAND)
U.S. ally, 1780

Cork

AUSTRIAN
NETHERLANDS

RANGER

London

Captured
MAYFLOWER

Sinks
DOLPHIN

Plymouth

Dunkirk

RANGER

GERMAN
STATES

Atlantic

BATTLE OF
USHANT,
July 27, 1778

English Channel

Ocean

BONHOMME RICHARD

Le Havre

Paris

Brest

St.Malo

FRENCH
INVASION
ARMY 31,000

L'Orient

Nantes

FRANCE
U.S. ally, 1778

Key

➤ Jones's voyages	🏳 Captured ship
RANGER American ship	⛵ Battle
DRAKE British ship	✴ Fleet Battle

*Bay of
Biscay*

Rochefort

0   150   300

Miles

Bordeaux

The *Ranger* versus the *Drake* off
the coast of Ireland in April 1778

Insert: Jones leading the raid
against Whitehaven, England

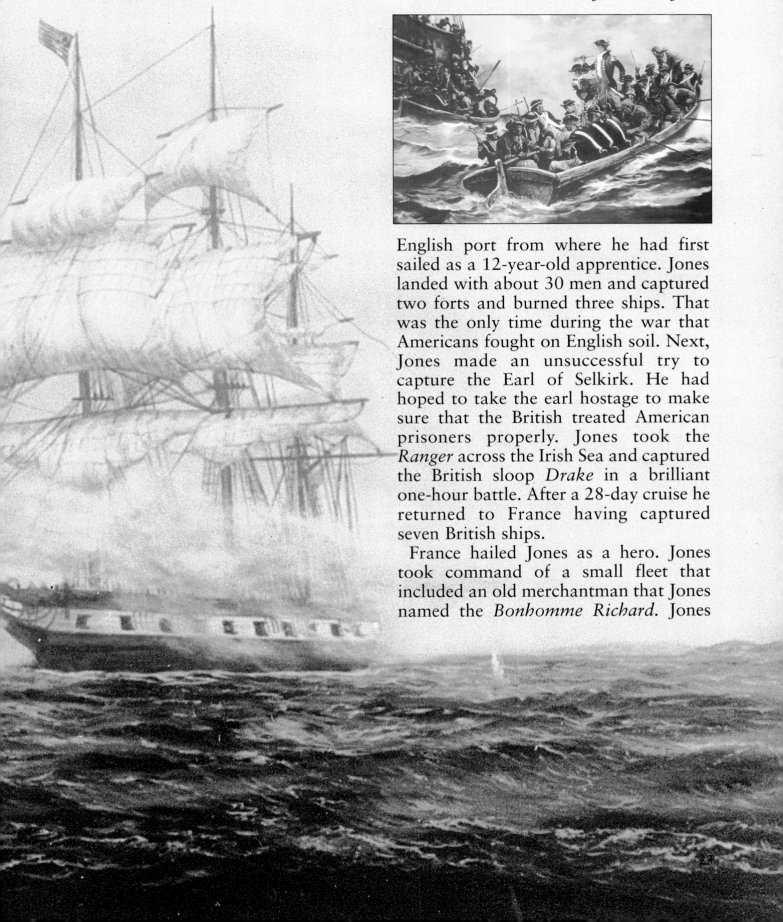

English port from where he had first sailed as a 12-year-old apprentice. Jones landed with about 30 men and captured two forts and burned three ships. That was the only time during the war that Americans fought on English soil. Next, Jones made an unsuccessful try to capture the Earl of Selkirk. He had hoped to take the earl hostage to make sure that the British treated American prisoners properly. Jones took the *Ranger* across the Irish Sea and captured the British sloop *Drake* in a brilliant one-hour battle. After a 28-day cruise he returned to France having captured seven British ships.

France hailed Jones as a hero. Jones took command of a small fleet that included an old merchantman that Jones named the *Bonhomme Richard*. Jones

Insert Above: Jones inspects the Continental Marines aboard his ship the *Bonhomme Richard*.

The *Serapis* burns during its battle against the *Bonhomme Richard*.

chose the name to honor his friend Ben Franklin who was the author of *Poor Richard's Almanac.* In 1779 *Poor Richard's Almanac* was popular in France under the French title *Les Maxime de Bonhomme Richard.* Jones sailed from France on August 14, 1779, for another raid around the British Isles. He captured 17 British ships and took their crews prisoner. Then, on September 23, 1779, Jones fought his most famous battle, against the British warship *Serapis.*

The battle began in the morning when Jones sighted two British warships escorting 40 British merchantmen near the English coast. For eight hours Jones chased the British warships, the *Serapis* with 44 guns and the *Countess of Scarborough* with 20 guns. Jones ordered three of his ships to attack the smaller British ship while he personally attacked the *Serapis.*

The *Bonhomme Richard* carried 42 guns including six 18-pounders (cannons were identified by the weight of the iron balls they fired). The *Serapis* and the *Bonhomme Richard* traded fire. Two of the *Bonhomme Richard's* 18-pounders accidently exploded. The gun crews of the other four 18-pounders were too frightened to fire their weapons because they worried that their guns might also explode. An American officer described the scene: The *Serapis* "raked us with whole broadsides [a broadside is the fire from all the cannons on one side of a ship] and showers of musketry. Several of her 18-pound shot having gone through our ship . . . made dreadful havock among our crew."

The battle was at such close range that the bow, or front, of the *Bonhomme Richard* ran up against the stern, or rear, of the *Serapis.* Jones's ship was in a terrible position, unable to move and unable to fire any of her guns. Because the *Bonhomme Richard* was not firing, the commander of the *Serapis,* Captain Richard Pearson, shouted out the question: "Has your ship struck [surrendered]?"

Jones replied with one of the most famous lines in American military history: "I have not yet begun to fight!"

The two ships separated and then came together again. Jones realized that he could not win by trading cannon fire because the British still had their 18-pounders, the

British crew was better trained to use their guns, and the *Serapis* turned faster than the *Bonhomme Richard*. So, Jones ordered his crew to lash, or tie, the ships together.

Now began a bloody fight at point-blank range. American sailors and marines, using muskets and small cannons, gained the advantage in the fight above the deck. But the British gained the advantage in the fight below the deck where the bigger guns continued to fire at one another. The British 18-pounders blew holes in the side of the *Bonhomme Richard* and knocked out her cannons one by one. Water poured into the *Bonhomme Richard,* and she slowly began to sink.

Jones directs the fighting from the deck of the *Bonhomme Richard.*

The battle between the *Bonhomme Richard* and the *Serapis* was the most famous naval action involving an American warship of the Revolutionary War.

29

One of Jones's other ships, the *Alliance*, now appeared. Jones related, "I thought the battle at an end (because reinforcements had arrived); but, to my utter astonishment, he discharged a broadside full into the stern of the *Bonhomme Richard*!" American officers yelled to the *Alliance* to stop firing, but the *Alliance* continued to punish the *Bonhomme Richard*. Only later would the Americans learn that the commander of the *Alliance*, a French officer named Pierre Landais, was so mentally unbalanced that people called him "mad."

The situation aboard the *Bonhomme Richard* was so bad that three American officers panicked. They freed all the British prisoners who had been captured in earlier battles and ran to the ship's flag to begin hauling it down as a sign of surrender. Jones ran at the three officers and made them stop. He bluffed the prisoners into believing that the *Bonhomme Richard* was about to sink unless

Marines fighting from their duty stations high in the masts of the *Bonhomme Richard*. One marine is about to throw a grenade.

the prisoners went below deck to man the pumps. Then Jones returned to command the battle against the *Serapis*.

An American sailor managed to drop a hand grenade onto the *Serapis*. The grenade landed on some gunpowder and caused an explosion. A British officer wrote: "It was awful! Some twenty of our men were fairly blown to pieces." Still, the gallant British captain rallied his men to continue the fight.

Jones had ordered his few surviving cannons to aim at the *Serapis*'s mainmast (a giant tree trunk supporting a ship's biggest sails). Finally, the damaged mainmast began to totter and threaten to fall. That helped convince Pearson to surrender the *Serapis*. But what really convinced Pearson was the fact that he could see, as he later wrote, that Jones was utterly determined to win the battle and "if he could not conquer, to sink alongside."

The *Bonhomme Richard* lost 49 killed and 67 wounded during the battle. The *Bonhomme Richard* sank from the battle damage two days after the fight. But the victory over the *Serapis* had been an amazing feat. An American historian described it as a "demonstration of superior seamanship and indomitable [refusing to admit defeat] fighting spirit."

The *Serapis* lost 54 killed and 75 wounded. Captain Pearson also received much credit from the fight because he had done his duty by sacrificing his ship to save his convoy.

After three years of service in Europe Jones returned to America in February 1781. Congress wanted to promote Jones to admiral, but other naval officers were jealous of him. They blocked his promotion. Instead, Jones received command of a new ship being built in Portsmouth, New Hampshire. It took a year to build the ship, and then Congress decided to give it to the French. Jones never again served in combat aboard an American ship.

From a British viewpoint Jones was "an ex-slaver turned pirate." From an American viewpoint he was the greatest naval hero of the war. After the Revolutionary War Catherine the Great of Russia hired Jones to serve in the Russian Navy. Jones died in 1792.

CHAPTER THREE

The Impact of the French

During the period 1775–1777 the Royal Navy did not have to worry about the rebel navy because the Continental Navy was too small to bother it very much. On March 13, 1778, the French ambassador in London told the British about the French alliance with the American rebels. France's entry into the war changed the war completely for Great Britain. British authorities immediately focused their attention on the likelihood of a war with France.

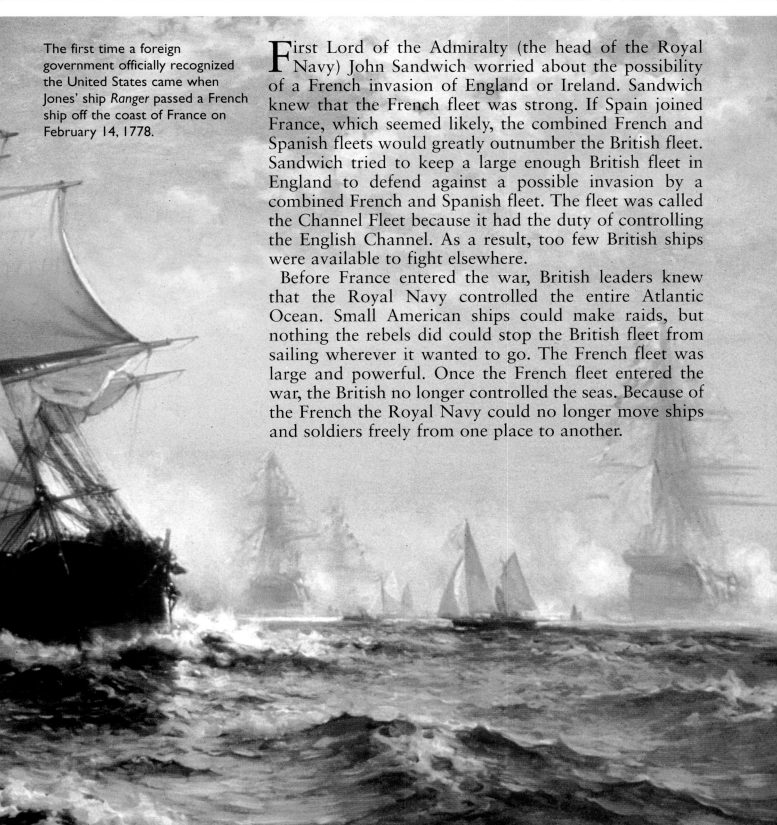

The first time a foreign government officially recognized the United States came when Jones' ship *Ranger* passed a French ship off the coast of France on February 14, 1778.

First Lord of the Admiralty (the head of the Royal Navy) John Sandwich worried about the possibility of a French invasion of England or Ireland. Sandwich knew that the French fleet was strong. If Spain joined France, which seemed likely, the combined French and Spanish fleets would greatly outnumber the British fleet. Sandwich tried to keep a large enough British fleet in England to defend against a possible invasion by a combined French and Spanish fleet. The fleet was called the Channel Fleet because it had the duty of controlling the English Channel. As a result, too few British ships were available to fight elsewhere.

Before France entered the war, British leaders knew that the Royal Navy controlled the entire Atlantic Ocean. Small American ships could make raids, but nothing the rebels did could stop the British fleet from sailing wherever it wanted to go. The French fleet was large and powerful. Once the French fleet entered the war, the British no longer controlled the seas. Because of the French the Royal Navy could no longer move ships and soldiers freely from one place to another.

Instead, British strategists had to worry about what might happen if a French fleet intercepted a British fleet. In any battle between large fleets the fight between the ships of the line decided who won and who lost. In order to have a good chance to win such a fight, a fleet needed to have about as many ships of the line as the enemy fleet had. So, naval strategists had to calculate how many enemy ships of the line their own fleet might have to face. Then, they had to make sure that their own fleet had about as many ships of the line as the enemy fleet.

During a battle on March 7, 1778, the American frigate *Randolph* was beating the more powerful British HMS *Yarmouth* when a lucky shot hit the *Randolph* and caused it to catch fire and explode.

The British Change Their American Strategy

News of the French alliance did not surprise the British government. However, it forced a change of strategy. Sandwich explained the new strategy to Lord Howe, the naval officer who commanded the Royal Navy in American waters: "The object of the war being now changed and the contest in America being secondary...our principal object must be distressing France and defending...His Majesty's possessions." England could not "distress" (bother) France by

Black Soldiers in the Revolution

When the Revolution began, about two million people lived in the colonies, and nearly half a million, or one person in four, were slaves of African descent. Both the British and the Continental forces needed all the men they could find. Neither side could overlook such a large part of the population.

Each of the rebellious states made its own rules about whether to include blacks, either slaves or free men, in their militia. For example, the New Hampshire militia included slaves who fought "with the Consent of their Masters." Massachusetts paid the owners for any of their slaves who enlisted. Connecticut allowed slaves to enlist as substitutes for their owners. Massachusetts, Connecticut, Rhode Island, and New York all accepted free blacks and recruited slaves. Some states offered freedom to slaves in exchange for their army service.

Slavery was far more prevalent in the southern colonies. Many southerners were unwilling to let their slaves join the army because they feared the slaves would escape. The South Carolina militia offered to pay owners to lend their slaves as laborers. Late in the war Maryland allowed slaves who had permission from their owners to enlist. Elsewhere in the south slaves were not allowed to join the army, but free blacks were drafted. In 1778, for example, there were 138 blacks serving with Virginia Continental units and 58 blacks in the North Carolina Continental units.

At first, the Continental Army did not allow blacks to join because the idea upset many white southerners. But by the end of 1775 General Washington decided that it made sense to recruit blacks. The army desperately needed men, and the British were offering freedom to slaves who joined the British army. The Continental Navy, state navies, and privateers allowed blacks to join them as sailors. Black sailors from the northern states were often free men who had worked on fishing boats. Southern black sailors were often slaves.

Most blacks served alongside whites in Continental army and navy units. There were three all-black units attached to the Continental Army. One of General Nathanael Greene's relatives, Colonel Christopher Greene, commanded the nearly all-black 1st Rhode Island Regiment, also called the Black Regiment of Rhode Island. Rhode Island recruited about 130 slaves for the regiment and paid their owners for their freedom. The regiment performed well in several battles. An officer with the French forces said of the regiment in 1781, "Three-quarters of the Rhode Island regiment consists of negroes, and that regiment is the most neatly dressed, the best under arms, and the most precise in its maneuvers."

A total of about 5,000 blacks served in American forces during the Revolution. Black American soldiers took part in many battles, especially in the north, including Lexington, Concord, Bunker Hill, Princeton, Brandywine, Newport, and Yorktown. After the Battle of Bunker Hill one black man received this praise: "We declare that a negro man named Salem Poor, . . . behaved like an experienced officer, as well as an excellent soldier. . . . In the person of this said negro, centers a brave and gallant soldier." Blacks also helped the cause in other ways, by serving as spies, guides, aides, servants, and bodyguards. William Lee, a slave, went through the entire war with George Washington. Another slave, James Armistead, served as a spy for Lafayette. The state of Virginia later bought him from his owner and freed him.

The British promised freedom to slaves if they would desert their owners and join the British side. Several thousand slaves accepted their offer and served the British army, mostly as laborers. Many worked at building the British defenses of Savannah and Augusta, Georgia. Blacks also worked for the British as spies, scouts, guides, pilots, wagon drivers, drummers, messengers, servants, cooks, and laundresses. Some served as fighting men in such units as the "Black Dragoons." The loyalist governor of Virginia reported to the British: "I have been [trying] to raise two regiments here—one of white people, the other of black. The [first] goes on very slowly, but the [last] very well." He recruited 300 black soldiers within a few weeks.

In addition, there were whole units that were not combat units, such as the Black Guides and Pioneers, that had white officers and black soldiers. In these units the black privates, corporals, and sergeants received the same pay as white infantrymen.

The British army used runaway slaves and free blacks for guerrilla warfare, night raids, and missions to collect food from the countryside. The British army also formed special units such as the "Negro Horse." The 100-man Negro Horse served in New York in 1782. It had the mission of patrolling near the city to stop British soldiers from deserting.

The German troops were less prejudiced toward blacks than were the British and attracted blacks as a result. Some American blacks moved to Germany after the war. More than 50,000 slaves (one-tenth of the black population) either escaped to British lines or were carried off by British military forces during the war.

During the war prejudice against blacks continued to be a problem. After the Revolution both sides failed to keep their promises to the blacks who had helped them fight the war. Some who stayed in America got captured and sold back into slavery. Thousands who escaped to British lines ended up in the West Indies and were forced back into slavery.

Soon after the war ended and men were no longer needed, the U.S. army and navy and the state militias stopped accepting blacks. Many black veterans had trouble getting their pensions after the war, on the grounds that they were runaway slaves.

The war caused people to think about the meaning of freedom. Some Americans turned against slavery. They believed that all people who had helped fight for the nation's freedom should be free. But many other Americans, especially in the South, continued to believe that slavery was right. The difference of opinion would cause the nation enormous problems and eventually lead to civil war.

At the Battle of Newport, Rhode Island, Hessians charged the 1st Rhode Island Regiment three times. A white soldier who saw the attacks said of the 1st Rhode Island, "three times did they successfully repel the assault, and thus preserve our army from capture. . . . They were brave, hardy troops."

invading France. The British army was too small, and a large part of it was involved in North America. But England could strike at French colonies. The most valuable were in the West Indies.

At the time of the Revolutionary War the islands of the West Indies were colonies of different European countries. Spain, France, and England had the greatest number of colonies in the West Indies. The island colonies produced many valuable products, the most important of which was sugar. England depended much more on trade with its colonies than did France. England's trade with the West Indies was especially important to the nation's economy. The West Indies were a rich prize, and both England and France wanted to control the islands. Most of the war's naval fighting took place in the West Indies. A British official wrote, "The war has and ever must be determined in the West Indies."

The climate and the weather influenced military activity in the West Indies. During the summer mosquitoes thrived on the islands. The mosquitoes carried deadly diseases, including malaria and yellow fever. People did not know that mosquitoes carried those diseases, but they did know that the summer was a time of sickness and death. Military leaders knew that many sailors and soldiers would die if they stayed in the West Indies during the summer. Then came the hurricane season in the late summer and early fall. Sailing ships could not survive hurricanes, and there was no way to predict exactly when the storms might strike. Strategists tried to avoid sending men and ships to the West Indies during the summer and early fall because of diseases and hurricanes.

Strategists realized that the best places to use their forces were along the American coast during the summer and the West Indies during the winter. For the rest of the war both the British and the French followed that pattern.

While making plans, the British leaders worried about what to do if and when the French sent a fleet across the Atlantic. British naval strategists tried to guess when a French fleet might sail, where it would go, and how big it would be. Then the British sent their own ships to match the French. The British were very good at making those guesses and taking the right steps to stop the French. But they could not be correct all of the time; and when they made mistakes, the French fleet had a big opportunity to accomplish something important.

The British had badly defeated the French during the battles of 1759 (which were part of the Seven Years' War, called the French and Indian War in America). Those battles had just about destroyed the French fleet. Ever since, for almost 20 years French dockyards had been conducting a massive rebuilding program. The French had built a powerful fleet of new ships. A typical new French warship was better than a typical older British warship.

The first opportunity for the new French fleet came in the spring of 1778. A large fleet commanded by Admiral Charles d'Estaing left Toulon, France, on April 13 and sailed for America. Because France was not yet at war with England, the British could not stop d'Estaing's fleet. If d'Estaing arrived on the American coast before the British were ready, his fleet could inflict terrible damage.

Continental Marines raise the American flag over a captured British fort in the Bahamas.

CHAPTER FOUR

The British Evacuate Philadelphia

The main British army, commanded by General William Howe, spent the winter of 1777–1778 in Philadelphia. Time passed very pleasantly for the British officers. Many wealthy loyalists (also called Tories) lived in the city. They were happy to serve as hosts for the men who were working to protect them from the rebels. In the words of one historian, "For the British officers, the occupation of Philadelphia was one continual party." The officers spent their time drinking, dancing, and gambling.

The conditions for the common British soldiers were less pleasant. Philadelphia was crowded. The streets were filled with garbage. It was hard for soldiers to find places to live and food to eat. Even the State House, where the rebels had signed the Declaration of Independence, became a barracks and a prison.

General Howe had become tired of the war. Both he and his brother, Admiral Richard Howe, had never agreed with the British government's decision to fight the Americans. By the beginning of 1778 General Howe could not see a way for the British to win the war. He sent his resignation from army command, and King George accepted it.

General Henry Clinton arrived in Philadelphia in May 1778 to replace General Howe. At that time the British army in the colonies, including Hessians and

Henry Clinton

Born in 1730, Henry Clinton grew up in New York. His father was the colony's royal governor. At the age of 21 he became an officer in the British army's elite Coldstream Guards. Clinton performed well during the Seven Years' War in Europe. After the war he served in Parliament. He enjoyed five years of very happy marriage. The death of his wife depressed him greatly.

Clinton came to Boston in May 1775. He immediately showed himself to be full of energy and ideas. However, he had great trouble getting along with other high-ranking British generals. In September 1775 Clinton became second in command to Howe. Clinton probably planned the British strategy that led to victory on Long Island in 1776. Afterward he became disgusted with Howe's leadership. On March 7, 1778, the British Secretary of State signed orders naming Clinton to replace Howe. Clinton continued as the senior British general in North American until 1782. Among all generals on either side only George Washington held a crucial command longer than Clinton.

Loyalists, numbered 33,756 men. That powerful force consisted of 19,530 men in Philadelphia, 10,456 in New York, and 3,770 in Rhode Island. But the day after Clinton arrived, a British warship brought news that France had allied herself openly with the American rebels. Because of the alliance Lord Germain, the British Secretary of State, sent Clinton new orders. Clinton was to abandon Philadelphia and take his army by water to New York City. Then, if necessary, he would abandon New York as well.

When British officers learned that General Howe was returning to England, they decided to arrange a dazzling farewell party. A captain named John Andre was in charge of organizing it. The party featured jousting competitions between men dressed as medieval knights. Women wore expensive silk dresses. The guests enjoyed music, dancing, fireworks, and a midnight feast. A total of 430 people sat down to a dinner of soup, chicken, ham, lamb, beef, veal, meat pies, salads, puddings, and sweets. It was probably the most lavish party ever held in America up to that time.

This expensive party shocked some people. There was a war going on. The poorer people of Philadelphia as well as most of the soldiers lacked basic supplies. The American army was not far away. Admiral Howe's secretary wrote, "Every man of Sense...was ashamed of the way of doing it."

Clinton Moves by Land

Clinton's orders told him to leave Philadelphia on ships and also to send reinforcements to the West Indies and to attack Georgia. Clinton decided to ignore some of the orders. He believed that there were not enough ships to take his army to New York and to take forces to the West Indies and Georgia. So, he decided to march his army 90 miles over land through New Jersey to New York City. That required detailed, careful planning. The most risky time would come when the army had to cross the Delaware River. Clinton worried that the rebels might attack while his army was divided with some forces in New Jersey and some still in Pennsylvania. So, he tried to keep his plans secret.

However, word spread that the British were planning to abandon Philadelphia. This was a disaster for the loyalists. When the city's Tories heard the news, they were

A well-dressed woman gets out of a hand-carried carriage to attend a ball in British-occupied Philadelphia.

43

badly frightened. They had publicly supported the British during the army's stay in Philadelphia. Now they were scared about what would happen when the rebels returned. Many believed that they would be hanged and all of their property including their homes and land taken from them. Joseph Galloway had served as General Howe's adviser and had run the city's civil government. Galloway knew that he would be a target for rebel revenge. He concluded that he had to flee and leave behind everything he owned. Galloway believed that in the future he would have to "wander like Cain upon the Earth without Home, & without Property."

Galloway was only one Philadelphia loyalist among thousands who had aided the British. Like Galloway, many chose safety, left with the army, and never saw Philadelphia again. Almost overnight they changed from the leading members of Philadelphia society to refugees. The evacuation of Philadelphia sent a hard lesson to loyalists all over America. They learned that they could not count on the British army for protection. People throughout the colonies who had been thinking about joining the king's cause decided they would be wise to wait.

Before dawn on June 16 the British began removing the artillery from the redoubts (defensive positions built from earth and timber) that guarded the city. That was the first step in the evacuation of Philadelphia. The same day some British infantry regiments crossed the Delaware River into New Jersey. The heaviest equipment, sick soldiers, and some 3,000 Tories who decided it was unsafe to stay in Philadelphia boarded ships. The next day the evacuation continued. By June 18 the army had successfully completed the dangerous task of evacuating the city and moving into New Jersey.

However, Clinton had assembled a huge wagon train to supply the army. The train stretched over nearly twelve miles of road and slowed the march. Clinton divided his army in two. He assigned the German General Knyphausen the task of guarding the train. General Cornwallis commanded the rear guard, the force given the dangerous duty of protecting the army if Washington attacked.

Washington's Army Leaves Valley Forge

The spring of 1778 marked the beginning of an easier time for the American army at Valley Forge. By working closely with Congress, Washington had managed to improve the army's Commissary Department (in charge of getting food) and Quartermaster Department (in charge of most other supplies). Food, which had been so scarce during the difficult winter, began arriving at Valley Forge. Warmer weather and more and better food

Spring at Valley Forge. Washington and his staff point to a wagon train that is bringing food for the soldiers.

improved the soldiers' health. A Rhode Island officer wrote to his wife: "I live very well...I rise with the sun. [after dressing] we begin our exercises [drill] at 6 o'clock which last till 8 in the morning. Then we breakfast upon tea or coffee." After breakfast the officers "walk, write, read, ride or play till dinner time, when we get a piece of good beef or pork . . . and we have as good bread as I ever eat." Army business, with drills and inspections, started up again at 5 P.M. and lasted until sunset. The officer concluded, "Our Regiment begins to grow healthy."

Washington reorganized the army to prepare it for a new campaign. He distributed the soldiers among five divisions. The most important command went to General Charles Lee. Lee had been captured back in

A reconstructed troop cabin at Valley Forge

1776 but had recently returned to the army. He was the army's senior general. Only Washington held a higher rank. Lee commanded the army's first **division.** The other divisional commanders were Thomas Mifflin, the Marquis de Lafayette, Johan DeKalb, and William Stirling.

During the spring Baron von Steuben continued with the army's training program. In the past, Continental units had experienced great trouble moving on a battlefield and working as a team. Because of von Steuben's training, entire divisions could maneuver together. Von Steuben made the Continentals nearly as good as the British regulars.

On May 5 a messenger from Congress arrived at Valley Forge to tell Washington that Congress had ratified the French alliance. Washington called for his entire army to parade the next day to celebrate the good news. The cannons started the celebration by firing a thirteen-gun salute in honor of the thirteen states. Then the infantry, who had formed in a long battle line two ranks deep, started "a running fire" of musketry from the right of the front line to the left. As soon as the last soldier on the left fired his musket, the man behind him fired, and then the running fire continued along the second rank from left back to the right. After everyone had fired, the soldiers cheered "Long Live the King of France."

Washington held high hopes that if his army cooperated with d'Estaing's French fleet, the war might be won in 1778. By late May George Washington knew that the British were preparing an operation, but he did not know exactly what. He decided to keep his army at Valley Forge until he knew for sure what the British were going to do. Even though the army had suffered terribly during the winter, it began the 1778 campaign in better shape than ever before. On June 12 Washington commanded 13,503 men. About 2,300 of them were sick and unfit for duty.

When Washington received definite news that the British were leaving Philadelphia, he called his generals to a council of war. Washington asked his generals whether the army should attack Clinton or let him escape. General Charles Lee had professional experience with the British army. Lee said that the American

> **division:** a large army unit usually made up of three or more brigades

Continentals could not stand up to the British in a battle. He concluded that the best choice was to let Clinton go. Many of the American generals greatly respected Lee and agreed. So Washington decided to move cautiously, and he missed a chance to damage the British while they were divided by the Delaware River. Not until June 23 did Washington allow his army to cross the Delaware River and chase the British.

Meanwhile, the first rebels returned to Philadelphia on June 18. They found that the British had destroyed or damaged many buildings, including churches that supported the rebel cause. The British left behind piles of filth and garbage in all the buildings they had used as barracks, hospitals, and stables. Rebel families who had fled the city returned to find that the British and Hessians had stolen most of their property. The rebels took revenge against the loyalists who remained in the city. The rebels decided that all loyalists who had helped the British or who had joined the British army or navy were guilty of treason. Their homes and land were taken from them as punishment.

In order to keep control in the city, Washington appointed an officer as military governor. In the past, General Benedict Arnold had always been very eager to lead at the front of a battle. Washington offered Arnold a command in his army, but Arnold declined. He said that the wound he had suffered at Saratoga still hurt him too much. So, Washington named Arnold military governor of Philadelphia. That proved to be a fateful step leading to Arnold's treason. While Arnold was in Philadelphia, he would meet and fall in love with a young and ambitious Tory woman named Margaret ("Peggy") Shippen.

Many men, including Benedict Arnold, considered Peggy Shippen a very attractive woman. Arnold worked hard to convince the young Tory to marry him.

48

CHAPTER FIVE

The Battle of Monmouth

Clinton's army marched north through New Jersey during terrible weather. Violent storms poured rain down on the army's head. The roads turned muddy, and creeks flooded.

American militia destroyed the bridges along the British route, forcing Clinton's men to take time to rebuild them. All of those things slowed the British march. Because the army had a baggage train of 1,500 wagons, it often marched only six miles during a day. The slow pace of the march gave Washington another chance to attack.

The machinery and equipment needed to move and operate a single cannon

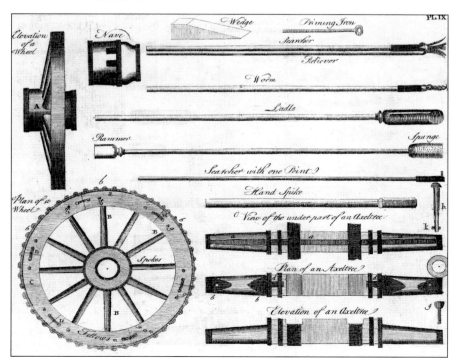

Douglas Freeman, who wrote a biography of Washington, described Washington's challenge: "The task of the American commander was simply stated but was difficult to [do]: He must use his outposts...in such a [way] that he would have a force on almost every road the British might use, and, at the same time, he must not so scatter his troopers that he would be unable to concentrate quickly when" the British plan became clear.

On June 24 Washington called another council of war. Again he asked if the army should attack Clinton. Again General Charles Lee argued that it would be "criminal" to risk a fight with the professional British soldiers. Again several other officers agreed with Lee. But Washington asked General Anthony Wayne what he thought should be done. Wayne answered simply, "Fight, sir!" Nathanael Greene, Lafayette, and John Cadwalader agreed with Wayne. But they were a minority, so Washington decided still to move cautiously. He ordered a small force of only 1,500 men to harass the British if they got a chance.

Then Washington received some new reports from his scouts that Clinton was marching toward Monmouth Court House. He changed his plan and decided to send a strong advance guard with almost half his army to harass the British. Washington ordered Lafayette to command the force. When Lee learned about it, he asked to be placed in command. Lee's request put Washington in a difficult situation. Washington knew that Lee did not think that the Americans could beat the British. But since Lee held such a high rank, his request could not easily be turned down. So Washington allowed Lee to take command of the advance guard.

Above: An enormous amount of baggage, such as this officer's camp chest which carried glass bottles and wine glasses, hindered the British march through New Jersey.

Left: General John Cadwalader was one of the officers who agreed with Anthony Wayne that the army should attack the British.

Lee and Washington

On June 26 General Clinton's army marched 19 miles to arrive at Monmouth Court House. The temperature was 100 degrees, the day humid, and the road deep with sand. The soldiers, wearing their wool uniforms and carrying heavy packs, were exhausted by the march. Clinton rested the army the next day.

Washington urging his men to march quickly in hopes of catching the British while Clinton is retreating through Monmouth Court House.

Washington was unsure about what Clinton intended to do. The situation was confused. American troops lay scattered all around Monmouth. Washington was with the main group of the army, about 7,000 men, while Lee commanded the force closest to the British. Washington still wanted to strike a blow before Clinton escaped back to New York. He sent reinforcements to Lee along with a message to attack the British rear. Lee

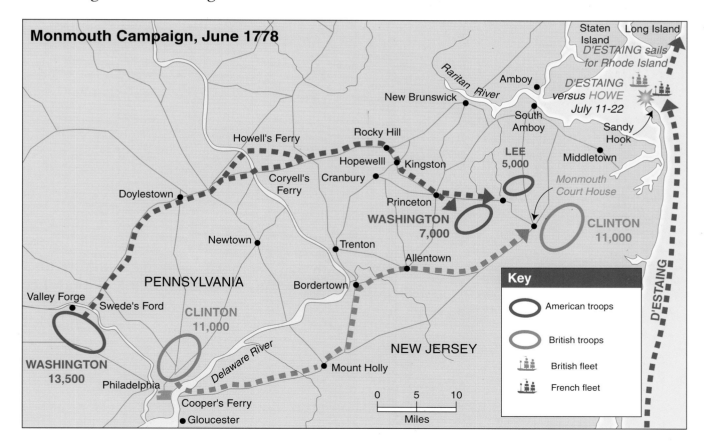

Monmouth Campaign, June 1778

Staten Island
Long Island
D'ESTAING sails for Rhode Island

D'ESTAING versus HOWE July 11-22

Raritan River

Amboy

New Brunswick

South Amboy

Sandy Hook

Rocky Hill

Howell's Ferry

Hopewelll
Kingston

LEE 5,000

Middletown

Coryell's Ferry
Cranbury

Monmouth Court House

Doylestown

Princeton

WASHINGTON 7,000

CLINTON 11,000

Newtown

Trenton

Allentown

PENNSYLVANIA

Bordertown

Valley Forge

Swede's Ford

CLINTON 11,000

Delaware River

NEW JERSEY

Mount Holly

WASHINGTON 13,500

Philadelphia

D'ESTAING

Cooper's Ferry

Gloucester

0   5   10
Miles

Key

⬭ American troops

◯ British troops

⛵ British fleet

⛵ French fleet

sent back a message that he expected the British to attack him instead! Lee was behaving too cautiously and was stubbornly resisting what Washington wanted.

On June 28 the German General Knyphausen continued the march of Clinton's baggage train and the Hessian soldiers at 4 A.M. Cornwallis remained behind to continue to guard the army's rear. One hour later Washington received a report about this march. Washington ordered his army to hurry ahead. The Americans were eager to fight. For many months at Valley Forge they had trained hard for just this battle. A Rhode Island captain told his men, "Now, you have been wishing for some days...to come up with the British, you have been wanting to fight,...now you shall have fighting enough before night."

Even though Lee was closer to the British, he did not begin his advance until 7 A.M. Lee failed to scout the ground leading to the British position. Then Lee became confused about whether the British were actually retreating. Lee did not realize that Knyphausen was retreating while Cornwallis was staying behind. Lee issued a series of orders to his men to attack Cornwallis. But the orders were so poor that soldiers first marched one way and then another until most of the American force became disorganized.

Clinton, who had stayed behind with Cornwallis, reacted quickly to Lee's blundering. He decided to attack the American right flank. Many of the American soldiers showed good discipline and kept their organization. But Lee's poor leadership and Clinton's skillful attack put some rebel units in bad situations, so they had to retreat. Seeing that some soldiers were falling back, other men began also to fall back. Lee gave up and ordered his entire force to retreat. A French volunteer who saw the American retreat wrote, "We were thoroughly beaten, our soldiers fled in the greatest disorder, and we could not succeed in rallying them, or even in getting thirty men to keep together."

The Americans retreated about three miles. At that point Washington rode up to his defeated soldiers. Washington could not understand why his fine army was retreating. He demanded an explanation from Lee. Lee was embarrassed. He said his forces had become

American soldiers charge to the attack.

Above: Washington tries to rally his soldiers during the early part of the Battle of Monmouth.

Below: Washington orders his men forward while one soldier (left in front) pauses for a drink of water.

disorganized, so he did not want to continue the fight. Besides, he added, he had never wanted to attack the British in the first place.

Washington lost his temper. He hotly said that whatever Lee wanted to do was not the point. Lee was a military man, and he was supposed to follow orders. While Lee sulked, Washington set out to rally the army so it could continue the fight. Washington rode forward to study the British position. A Continental soldier saw that Washington "remained there some time upon his old English charger, while the shot from the British artillery were rending up the earth all around him. After he had taken a view of the enemy, he returned and ordered the two Connecticut brigades to make a stand at

a fence, in order to keep the enemy in check" while Lee's men retreated behind a deep ravine called the West Ravine.

Washington next organized a defensive force behind the West Ravine to stop the British if they kept attacking. Washington took advantage of the fact that one of his New Jersey officers knew the local land. The officer gave advice about how Washington could best arrange his forces.

Clinton first attacked Washington's left, then his right, and finally his center. Washington, Steuben, and Stirling rode among the rebels to encourage the infantry to stand firm. As at the Battle of Princeton (January 2, 1777; see Volume 4) Washington's "fine appearance" and "calm courage" rallied his men. Other officers, including Henry Knox and Nathanael Greene, positioned the American artillery in excellent positions so their fire could help the infantry.

In the final British attack the best soldiers in the British army charged the American center. Anthony Wayne commanded the Americans in the center. Twice his men repulsed the British grenadiers, foot guards, light infantry, and regulars. A British Colonel, Henry Monckton, rallied his men for a third charge, "Forward to the charge, my brave grenadiers!"

Wayne told his men, "Steady! steady! Wait for the word, then pick out the king-birds!" [meaning shoot at the officers]. The Americans fired at point-blank range. Colonel Monckton fell with a mortal wound just in front of the rebel line. Many of his men were also hit, and the charge failed.

It was now about 5 P.M. The armies had fought to a standstill. The soldiers on both sides suffered terribly from the day's heat and humidity. A Continental soldier

Two gallant young officers, one British and one American, fight a duel between the lines while nearby soldiers watch.

wrote, "The weather was almost too hot to live in." Men on both sides were exhausted and desperately thirsty. Washington tried to get some of his reinforcements to attack, but the soldiers collapsed from fatigue. So the Battle of Monmouth ended in a draw.

The Americans lost 356 men, including 37 who probably died from sunstroke. British losses are uncertain, but they were probably higher and included about 60 men who died of sunstroke. Both armies slept on the battlefield. Before dawn Clinton slipped away to finish the march to New York City.

Monmouth was the last important battle in the north. The British army had fought in its usual brave and professional manner. Washington's army did better than it had ever done before. Less than one year earlier the rebel army had badly lost the Battle of Brandywine. During that battle regiments had been unable to maneuver while under fire. It was different at Monmouth. There the Americans showed how much they had learned from Steuben's training at Valley Forge.

The rebels had become confused during the morning battle. But that was entirely Charles Lee's fault. After the battle Lee requested a court martial (a military trial). Numerous witnesses testified that Lee had

A thirsty soldier dips his hat in a pool of water while his unit hurries forward.

shown personal courage. But they also said that Lee did not follow orders to attack the British, and then he lost control of his men when the fight began. The court judged Lee guilty and sentenced him to a 12-month suspension from command. Lee never again held any other command. The rebel army was better off without him.

In three years of war Washington had failed to defeat the British in a large battle. However, he had prevented a much stronger British army from conquering the rebellious colonies, and he had forced that army to return to its base in New York City. In other words, the main British army was back where it had started from in 1776.

Several patriotic women brought water to the thirsty soldiers during the Battle of Monmouth. The legend of Molly Pitcher is probably based on Mary Ludwig Hays whose husband was in an artillery unit. Hays brought her husband and his crew water until late in the battle, when her husband fell wounded. She grabbed a rammer and took his place at his gun.

CHAPTER FIVE

The British Turn South

D'Estaing's fleet, which had left France in April 1778, made a very slow passage across the Atlantic. The voyage took 87 days. D'Estaing finally arrived off the American coast on July 8.

By that time the British had completed their move to New York. Washington and d'Estaing agreed on a plan to attack New York City. The French fleet sailed to New York City, where it found Admiral Howe's fleet defending the harbor. The French outnumbered the British in the all-important number of ships of the line.

The French fleet maneuvers off New York, while in the distance Lord Howe's British fleet waits behind the sandbar off Sandy Hook.

Plus, the French ships were fresh out of the dockyard. They were well equipped and could sail faster than the British ships. (When wooden-hulled sailing ships were at sea for a long time, great masses of seaweed attached to the hull and seriously slowed down the ships.)

However, the commander of the British fleet, Admiral Richard Howe, was an excellent tactician. Howe anchored his ships off Sandy Hook in such a way that their guns controlled the entrance to New York Harbor. In order to attack, the French had to cross a sandbar that ran from Staten Island to Sandy Hook. Rather than risk crossing the bar while facing Howe's guns, d'Estaing decided to head for Rhode Island to attack the British at Newport.

The idea of attacking Newport came from the Continental Congress. Congressmen thought that American soldiers led by General John Sullivan could cooperate with the French and recapture the port. George Washington agreed. He ordered 5,000 New England militia to assemble for the attack and sent some of his own Continentals marching north to Newport to help. Washington also sent two of his best leaders, Nathanael Greene, who was a native of Rhode Island, and Lafayette.

Admiral Richard Howe never thought that the war against the American rebels was wise policy for Great Britain. But he was a skilled professional sailor and showed his talents whenever he fought Great Britain's traditional enemy, France.

The French fleet reached Rhode Island on July 29, 1778. D'Estaing made contact with Sullivan in order to work out plans to cooperate against Newport. But Sullivan and d'Estaing did not get along. Sullivan tried to issue orders to the French admiral, and the Frenchman thought his behavior was inappropriate. Still, d'Estaing agreed to a plan in which his fleet would attack the west side of Newport while Sullivan's men attacked the east side. The attack began on August 8. By that time Sullivan had assembled more than 10,000 men. The British defenders had only about 3,000 men. It seemed like the capture of Newport was a sure thing. Instead, Howe's fleet appeared just at the time the French ships were involved in a difficult maneuver.

Back in June the Admiralty had learned that d'Estaing's fleet was sailing across the Atlantic. The Admiralty sent four ships of the line to reinforce Howe. Even though that still left Howe with a fleet only two-thirds the size of the French fleet, Howe boldly left New York to sail to Newport.

When d'Estaing saw Howe's fleet arrive off Newport, he decided to stop his efforts to cooperate with Sullivan and instead attacked the British fleet. For 24 hours the two fleets maneuvered carefully, each trying to gain an advantage. On the night of August 11 a violent storm struck. D'Estaing's **flagship,** the mighty 90-gun *Languedoc,* lost all of its masts and its rudder. Many

flagship: the ship used by an admiral as his head-quarters ship, identified by a flag

During storms like the one that struck the fleets off Rhode Island, sailors had to struggle to furl (take in and fold) the huge sails.

other ships on both sides received serious damage. Both fleets left Rhode Island for a safe harbor, the British returning to New York and the French sailing to Boston.

At Newport Sullivan tried to continue without the French. But the departure of the French discouraged the militia, and hundreds left the army. Finally, on August 28 Sullivan ordered a retreat. Sullivan and his generals wrote a letter blaming d'Estaing for the failure. Their letter caused a great deal of bad feeling between the Americans and the French. George Washington had to work hard to soothe hurt French feelings.

When Congress had ratified the French alliance on May 4, 1778, American patriots hoped that everything would quickly change for the better. In fact, too many rebels became overconfident. Some thought that when the French joined the rebel forces, the allies would soon defeat the British. Others thought that maybe they did not have to work so hard and sacrifice so much to win the war because now the French would do a great deal of the work. The events of 1778 showed that there were many problems to solve before the Americans and the French could work well together.

The failed Newport campaign ended any hopes that the French alliance would bring an early victory over the British. On November 4, 1778, d'Estaing left Boston for the West Indies. Once again British forces were free to sail wherever they wanted along the American coast. All the rebels could do was wait to see where the British would strike.

A Rhode Island artilleryman

A New British Strategy

In 1776 and 1777 the British military goal was to break the rebellion by crushing the rebel army and capturing the important cities. Those campaigns had failed. An increasing number of British politicians protested against the war. They said that Britain should abandon the war against America and concentrate on fighting France. Even Lord North complained that the objects of the war were not worth the cost.

King George disagreed strongly. He said that a powerful nation like Great Britain should not consider the cost of doing what needed to be done. The king said that Lord North's attitude was like "a tradesman behind his counter" weighing goods and deciding what to pay. The king deeply believed that there were more important issues than the cost of the war. He said that if Britain allowed the American rebels to win, then there would be revolts elsewhere until the entire British empire was lost.

British strategists always hoped to encourage the American loyalists to join the British army and help fight the rebels. But the loyalists had been reluctant to risk joining the British until they were sure that the British would stay to protect them. Too many times in the past the British had entered an area, the loyalists had declared their support for the king, the British had left, and the rebels had taken revenge on the loyalists. The most recent example had been in Philadelphia. A British admiral noted that the army's motion was like "the

The Continental Navy was too small to interfere seriously with British naval movements. Still, American warships won some victories. Here a Continental brig (the large ship in the middle) leads a captured British warship (on the left with its flag flying upside down as a symbol of its defeat) back to port in New England.

passage of a ship through the sea whose track is soon lost." In other words, the British presence in any one place had not lasted long enough for the loyalists to feel confident that they could support the king's forces.

Some British strategists argued that Great Britain had been following the wrong strategy since the beginning of the war. They noted that the rebellion was strongest in New England. It was a mistake to attack where the enemy was strongest. Instead, they suggested attacking the southern colonies. The southern colonies had far fewer people than the northern colonies. About 750,000 white people lived in Maryland, Virginia, North and South Carolina, and Georgia. About 300,000 black slaves also lived there. Southerners lived in fear of a slave revolt. Many white men of military age had to stay at home to guard the slaves. For those reasons there were fewer militia in the southern colonies. Also, British leaders believed that there were many loyalists in the southern colonies. They were just waiting for the British army to appear before rallying to support the king. Finally, the south's economy depended on exporting its farm goods. The British believed that rich southern farmers were eager for peace so that they could resume their exports.

In June 1776 the American defenders of Fort Moultrie defeated the first British attempt to capture Charleston, South Carolina.

The other advantage of making the main effort in the south was that it was closer to the West Indies. The British fleet had to keep a large force in the West Indies to guard against the French. British strategists believed that the fleet could support the effort to reconquer the southern colonies. Also, the British colonies in the West Indies imported food. The southern colonies grew enough food for export. After the British recaptured the southern colonies, the food could be used to feed the West Indian colonies.

The British had much practice and used a very professional approach for landing men from the sea. On a smaller scale (fewer men, fewer boats) the Americans followed the same procedures. Here rebel sailors land their boats through the surf while the warships wait offshore.

The basic British plan called for invading Georgia first. After conquering Georgia, the army would move north to capture the other southern colonies one by one. The rebels would be trapped: On the east was the Atlantic Ocean, dominated by the Royal Navy; on the west was the wilderness, dominated by the Indians; the British Army would move from the south to squeeze the rebels against the barrier formed by the main British army in New York City.

The Campaign Begins

When the war began, the British controlled East Florida. In 1776 the British commander of East Florida, Major General Augustine Prevost, ordered a fort to be built on the St. Mary's River. The river marked the southern border of Georgia. The fort, named Fort St. George, served as a base for British and Tory forces to raid north into Georgia.

In the summer of 1778 the American commander in the south, Major General Robert Howe, led a small rebel army against Fort St. George. Howe's army marched through a coastal area where very few people lived. The army's horses died of starvation. The soldiers suffered from the intense heat of coastal Georgia, and many fell sick. Malaria, yellow fever, and dysentery killed hundreds of men. The army's leaders fell to arguing about what to do. Finally, Howe ordered a retreat. Even though the army had not fought a battle, it had still lost 500 men to disease. That loss left Howe in poor shape to defend against the next British blow.

In November 1778 General Clinton ordered a 3,000-man force commanded by Lieutenant Colonel Archibald Campbell to sail from New York to Georgia. Campbell's little army landed outside of Savannah, Georgia, on December 29. Howe had only 700 men, mostly militia, to defend the city. Howe should have retreated, but he instead chose to stay and fight.

When the British sent powerful forces to invade the south, Congress sent Major General Benjamin Lincoln to command the Southern Department.

Campbell was a skilled soldier. He correctly judged that his best move was to attack quickly before the Americans received reinforcements. But first he carefully scouted Howe's position. A black slave showed him a path through a swamp that led to the rear of the rebel position. The slave guided Campbell's elite light infantry and a loyalist regiment, the New York Volunteers, along the path. Meanwhile, Campbell ordered the rest of his force to make a feint, or fake attack, against the American front in order to distract Howe's attention.

Campbell's plan worked perfectly. Howe's defenders faced an attack from the front and rear at the same time. After a few minutes of desperate fighting the rebels routed. Howe himself escaped, but his army lost 550 men killed or captured and all of its artillery. Campbell lost only 7 killed and 19 wounded. It was a small price to pay for Savannah, Georgia's largest, most important city.

Savannah served as a base for the British drive to capture all of Georgia. Over the next months Campbell cooperated with Prevost's force in Florida to secure most of the state. Most of the people living in eastern Georgia, the wealthiest and most productive part of the state, took the oath of allegiance to King George. The British began organizing them into loyalist military units. Elsewhere, in Georgia and the Carolinas, people heard the news of the British capture of Savannah. Loyalists began to gather to march to join the British in Georgia.

When Congress realized that the British had shifted their effort to the south, they sent Major General Benjamin Lincoln to replace Robert Howe as the commander in the Southern Department. Lincoln had dealt with difficult situations in the past. During the Bennington campaign in 1777 he had shown an ability to cooperate with other generals and work for the common good. He had been badly wounded at the Battle of Saratoga and had taken ten months to heal. He now walked with a permanent limp.

Lincoln arrived in Charleston, South Carolina, in December 1778. He found only 1,500 soldiers ready to march to try to save Savannah. Lincoln called out the militia and managed to increase his army to 3,500 men. By the time he was ready to march south, it was too late, the British had already captured Savannah. So, Lincoln moved his army to the South Carolina-Georgia border. Prevost, who was higher ranking than Campbell and had taken command of all British forces in the area, moved his British army to block Lincoln. The two armies faced one another across the wide Savannah River.

Because southern winters were mild, unlike in the north, military forces continued to march and fight during the winter months. In January 1779 Prevost sent Campbell with a force up the Savannah River toward Augusta. The object was to show the British flag and attract more recruits for the king's forces. Until now everything had gone smoothly for the British. But a South Carolina militia officer, Colonel Andrew Pickens, gathered a rebel force to stop the British move into western Georgia.

On January 29 Campbell captured Augusta. He left a Tory force to defend the town and moved on to secure western Georgia. At the same time, another force of 700 North Carolina loyalists led by Colonel James Boyd marched toward Augusta to join Campbell. Even though he commanded only about 300 men, Pickens decided that Boyd's men could be trapped and destroyed if the rebels moved quickly.

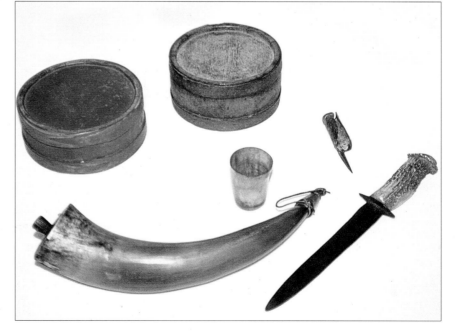

Some of the simple, basic equipment carried by rebel soldiers: canteens, powder horn, cup, knife.

On the morning of February 14, 1779, Pickens led a surprise attack against Boyd's Tories, who were camped at Kettle Creek. In less than an hour the rebels killed, captured, or scattered the Tories. Boyd suffered a mortal wound, and about 40 of his men were killed in the battle. The rebels lost about 30 men. Kettle Creek had been a fight between Americans. Like many such battles, this one turned savage. The rebels convicted all the Tory prisoners of

Colonel Andrew Pickens was one of the most skilled leaders of rebel militia in the south.

treason against the rebel cause and hanged five of them.

Like the Battles of Great Bridge (December 9, 1775) and Moore's Creek (February 27, 1776; see Volume 3), Kettle Creek had an important influence on the future. The Tories again learned that it was dangerous to rally for King George unless and until a powerful British force was present. So, most Tories in the south stayed home for a long time after that battle. On the other hand, patriot militia took heart from the battle. They gathered at Lincoln's camp and gave Lincoln the strength to try to recapture Georgia. He would begin his campaign in late January 1779.

Year in Review

The year 1778 had seen enormous changes. Burgoyne's surrender at Saratoga in 1777 ended the British effort to conquer the northern and middle colonies. The evacuation of Philadelphia marked the end of the plan to defeat the rebels by occupying their largest cities. British leaders including King George III realized that they had to make a new plan. The best chance for victory was to fight a limited war to grind down the rebels. That war began with the invasion of Georgia. British leaders hoped that eventually the Americans would grow tired of the war.

For the Americans the year had begun with high hopes that the French alliance would bring quick victory. But d'Estaing had come to America and had left, and nothing had been accomplished. George Washington firmly believed that with French help the rebels could win independence if they kept trying. After the frustrations of 1778 he feared that too many Americans were unwilling to make the sacrifices necessary to win the war. Many Americans were growing tired of the war, and Washington knew it.

Chronology

November 10, 1775: The Continental Congress creates the Marine Corps.

November–December 1775: Congress acts to buy and equip ships for the Continental Navy.

March 3–4, 1776: In their first battle the newly created Marine Corps captures a British fort on the coast of Nassau, in the West Indies.

April 13, 1778: Admiral Charles d'Estaing and the French fleet depart France for America.

April 28, 1778: Captain John Paul Jones of the Continental sloop *Ranger* raids Whitehaven, a British port.

May 1778: Henry Clinton arrives in Philadelphia to replace William Howe, who has resigned as commander of the British army in America.

May 4, 1778: The Continental Congress ratifies the French alliance.

June 16–18, 1778: Henry Clinton and the British army abandon Philadelphia and enter New Jersey.

June 28, 1778: George Washington's men fight Clinton's army to a draw at the Battle of Monmouth Court House.

July 8, 1778: Admiral d'Estaing and the French fleet arrive off the American coast.

August 8, 1778: American soldiers and the French fleet attack Newport, Rhode Island. The British fleet arrives and engages the French fleet. The two fleets fight without important results and scatter because of a storm, leaving the Americans to try to take Newport on their own.

August 28, 1778: The Americans retreat from Newport.

November 4, 1778: D'Estaing and the French fleet leave North America for the West Indies.

December 29, 1778: The British capture Savannah, Georgia.

January 29, 1779: The British capture Augusta, Georgia.

February 14, 1779: A patriot force surprises and routs twice as many Tories at Kettle Creek in Georgia. They hang five captured Tories as traitors.

September 23, 1779: John Paul Jones aboard the *Bonhomme Richard* forces England's *Serapis* to surrender after an epic sea battle.

Glossary

AGE OF SAIL: the period of history before engines were invented, when ships used sails to move across the water

ALLIANCE: an agreement between nations to fight on the same side in a war

ATTRITION: gradual wearing down; in war wearing down the enemy's will to continue the war by stubbornly fighting at every opportunity

CONVOY: several ships that travel together for protection

COUNCIL OF WAR: meeting of officers to decide on how to fight

COURT MARTIAL: trial by a military, or martial, court

DIVISION: a large army unit usually made up of three or more brigades

ELITE: special, or select; in the military specially chosen and trained fighters

FLAGSHIP: the ship used by an admiral as his headquarters ship, identified by a flag

FRIGATE: a medium-sized, fast-moving armed sailing ship

MAN-OF-WAR: warship

MARINES: troops equipped to fight either at sea or on land

MERCHANTMAN: trading ship

PRESS GANGS: groups of armed sailors who forced men to serve on their ships

PRIVATEER: privately owned ship with government permission to capture enemy ships and their cargos

RATIFY: vote to approve

REINFORCEMENTS: additional soldiers sent to help an army either before or during a battle

SHIP OF THE LINE: a warship large enough to be part of a line of battle

SLOOP: small armed sailing ship

TACTICS: the positioning of forces to fight a battle. A tactician is an expert in tactics.

TORY: someone who sided with Great Britain during the American Revolution; taken from the name of a political party in England

WEST INDIES: the islands of the Caribbean Sea, so called because they were once thought to be a part of India

Further Resources

Books:

Adams, Russell B., Jr., ed. *The Revolutionaries*. Alexandria, VA: Time-Life Books, 1996.

Bliven, Bruce, Jr. *The American Revolution*. New York: Random House, 1986.

Boatner, Mark M., III. *Encyclopedia of the American Revolution*. Mechanicsburg, PA: Stackpole Books, 1994.

Collier, Christopher and James Lincoln Collier. *The American Revolution, 1763–1783*. Tarrytown, NY: Marshall Cavendish Corp., 1998.

Cox, Clinton. *Come All You Brave Soldiers: Blacks in the Revolutionary War*. New York: Scholastic Press, 1999.

Dolan, Edward F. *The American Revolution: How We Fought the War of Independence*. Brookfield, CT: Millbrook Press, 1995.

Rankin, Hugh F., ed. *Narratives of the American Revolution as told by a young sailor, a home-sick surgeon, a French volunteer, and a German general's wife*. Chicago: Lakeside Press, 1976.

Scheer, George F. and Hugh F. Rankin. *Rebels & Redcoats: The American Revolution through the Eyes of Those Who Fought & Lived It*. New York: Da Capo Press, 1987.

Wilbur, C. Keith. *Pirates & Patriots of the American Revolution: An Illustrated Encyclopedia of Colonial Seamanship*. Old Saybrook, CT: Globe Pequot Press, 1984.

Websites

http://library.thinkquest.org/10966/
The Revolutionary War—A Journey Towards Freedom

ushistory.org/march/index.html
Virtual Marching Tour of the American Revolution

http://www.pbs.org/ktca/liberty/game/index.html
The Road to Revolution-A Revolutionary Game

http://www.pbs.org/ktca/liberty/chronicle/index.html
Chronicle of the Revolution
Read virtual newspapers of the Revolutionary era

A Place to Visit:

Mariners' Museum, Newport News, Virginia

About the Authors

James R. Arnold has written more than 20 books on military history topics and contributed to many others. Roberta Wiener has coauthored several books with Mr. Arnold and edited numerous educational books, including a children's encyclopedia. They live and farm in Virginia.

Set Index

Bold numbers refer to volumes; *italics* refer to illustrations

Acland, John **5:** 60–61
Acland, Lady Harriet **5:** *61*
Adams, Abigail **10:** 60
Adams, John **1:** 44, 56, 60; **2:** 46, 51–*52*; **3:** 60, 62; **4:** 16, 29–*30*, 44; **6:** 21, *29*, 43; **7:** 13, 15; **10:** 31, 39, *60*
Adams, John Quincy **10:** 60
Adams, Samuel **1:** 41, 44, 51–53, 57–58; **2:** 7, 19, 24–25, 51; **3:** 60; **6:** 43
Africa **10:** 25–27, 53
African Americans **2:** 53; **3:** 48, 64; **4:** 55; **7:** 36–37, 66; **10:** 44–47
    Armistead, James **7:** 36
    Lee, William **7:** 36
    Poor, Salem **7:** 36
    Slaves **7:** 36–37, 63; **8:** 50, 64; **10:** 25, 44, 46–47, 53
    Turner, Nat **10:** 46
    Whipple, Prince **4:** 55
Alexander, William (Lord Stirling) **4:** *24*, 27; **7:** 47, *55*
Allegheny Mountains **1:** 21, 22, 37, 55; **10:** 38, 42, 50
Allen, Ethan **1:** 31; **2:** 47, 50–*51*; **3:** 28–29
André, John **6:** 31; **7:** 41; **9:** 12–15
Armistead, James **7:** 36
Armstrong, John **6:** 24
Army organization **3:** 16–19
    Infantry **3:** 16–19
Army, standing **4:** 44–45; **10:** 28, 31, 39
Arnold, Benedict **1:** 31; **2:** 50; **3:** 26, 30–35; **4:** 15–19, 21, 66; **5:** 26, 44–45, 48, 51, 53, 55, 58, 60–63; **7:** 48; **9:** *10*–15; **10:** 11, 57, *60*
Arnold, Peggy (Shippen) **7:** *48*; **10:** 60
Articles of Confederation **10:** 38–39
Artillery; see also Weapons **1:** 25; **3:** 22–23, *38–41*; **4:** 26, 56; **5:** 29, 60, 63; **6:** 28, 41; **7:** 55; **9:** 50, 54–55; **10:** 18–19
Attucks, Crispus **1:** 45

Balfour, Nisbet **9:** 64
Bancroft, Edward **5:** 13
Barras, Jacques **10:** 15

Battle formation **2:** 49; **8:** 64; **9:** 34
Baum, Friedrich **5:** 33–36
Bayonets; see Weapons
Bemis Heights (N.Y.), battle **5:** 58–63
Bennington (Vt.), battle **5:** 33–39, 45–46, 48
Blacks; see African Americans
Blockades **3:** 64; **4:** 13–14, 21, 65–66; **6:** 66
Bonhomme Richard vs. *Serapis* **7:** 23–31
Boone, Daniel **8:** 8, 11
Boston Massacre **1:** *43–47*; **3:** 37
Boston (Mass.), siege **3:** 36–45; **7:** 11
Boston Tea Party **1:** *51*, *52–53*, 54–55, 57; **2:** 16, 18
Boycotts **1:** 42, 44–45, 57
Boyd, James **7:** 67
Braddock, Edward **1:** 19, 24–25, *28*
Brandywine (Pa.), battle **6:** 18, 22–28, 36; **7:** 56
Brant, Joseph **5:** 41; **8:** *21–22*; **10:** 48
Breymann, Heinrich **5:** 35–36, 62–63
Breed's Hill; see Bunker Hill
British armed forces **1:** 24–26, 28, 31, 34–35, *36–37*, 42–43, 62–63; **2:** 6–7, *17–18*, 43, 49, 55; **3:** 8, 14; **4:** 11; **6:** 8; **7:** 40; **8:** 46, 65; **9:** 38; **10:** 25, 32–33, 51, 57
    African Americans **7:** 37
    Dragoons **4:** 49; **9:** 35–36, *38–39*
    Grenadiers **2:** *19*, 22, 36–37, 61, 63; **3:** 49; **6:** *25*; **7:** 55
    Light infantry **2:** 12, 22, 28, 36–37, 63; **4:** 34; **6:** 38; **7:** 55, 66
    Scottish Highlanders **3:** *9*, 50–52; **4:** 34, *36*; **9:** 36, 39, 42
    Strength **3:** 28, 31, 44, 46, 51; **4:** 11–12, 14–15, 38–39, 43, 48; **5:** 39–40, 45, 48, 50–51, 56, 58; **6:** 12, 24, 36; **7:** 40–41, 60, 65; **8:** 29, 34, 46, 49; **9:** 30–31, 36, 58, 65; **10:** 12, 21
British Empire **1:** 14–16, 46, 49; **5:** 7; **7:** 62
British government **1:** 14–16; **3:** 6–7; **4:** 10–12; **5:** 6, 8; **7:** 6, 8; **8:** 6
British laws
    Boston Port Act **1:** 54, 57; **2:** 12, 19
    Declaratory Act **1:** 42
    Intolerable Acts **1:** 56, 59, 60
    Quartering Act **1:** 43, 55; **2:** 13
    Quebec Act **1:** 55–56
    Stamp Act **1:** 39–42
    Sugar Act **1:** 37–38

Tea Act **1:** 50
Townsend Revenue Act **1:** 42, 45
Brown, Thaddeus **2:** 27
Brown, Thomas **8:** 61; **9:** 63–64
Buford, Abraham **8:** 54, 64
Bunker Hill (Mass.), battle **2:** 53–66; **3:** 6–7, 13, 38; **4:** 38; **5:** 29
Burgoyne, John **2:** 55, 65; **3:** 10; **4:** 15; **5:** 8–11, 14–16, 18–21, 23–33, 39–40, 43, 45–48, 50, 54–58, 60, 63–65; **6:** *16*–17, 43, 63, 66; **7:** 68; **10:** 19, 66
Burr, Aaron **3:** 34; **4:** 33–34; **10:** 62
Burke, Edmund **1:** 46–47; **3:** *8–9*
Butler, John **8:** 18–19
Butler, Walter **8:** 19, 22

Cadwalader, John **4:** 52–53, 59, 66; **7:** *50*
Camden (S.C.), battle **8:** *56*–60, 65, 67; **9:** 10, 16–17, 26, 32, 38, 47
Campbell, Archibald **7:** 65–67; **8:** 27
Campbell, William **9:** 47
Canada **1:** 20–21, 29, 34–35, 36, 55–56; **4:** 14–17; **5:** 7–10, 12, 14, 18, 29, 46, 56; **6:** 9, 16; **8:** 6, 18–19; **10:** 49–50, 53
    Halifax **3:** 45; **4:** 6, 22; **8:** 40
    Invasion of **3:** 23–35; **4:** 15–17; **10:** 57
    Louisbourg **1:** 18, *34–35*; **3:** *24–25*
    Montreal **3:** 26, 29; **4:** 15
    Quebec **1:** 20, 35; **3:** 26, 29–35; **4:** 15
    St. Johns **3:** 28–29; **4:** 17
Cannons; see Weapons
Carleton, Guy **3:** 24, 28; **4:** 15, 17–18, 20; **5:** 7–8, 14, 18, 46; **10:** 24–25
Casualties **1:** 26, 28; **2:** 34–35, 44, 66; **3:** 35, 44, 49, 52, 59; **4:** 29, 35, 43, 56, 62; **5:** 36, 54, 63; **6:** 28, 31, 40, 42; **7:** 31, 56, 66–67; **8:** 25, 28, 31, 38–39, 42, 53, 59, 64; **9:** 24, 42, 49, 56–57, 62, 64–65, 68; **10:** 21
Caswell, Richard **2:** 51
Cavalry **3:** 20–22; **5:** 33; **6:** 24–25; **8:** 52, 54, 64; **9:** 35, 40–41, 46, 54
Champe, John **9:** 15
Charleston (S.C.), siege **8:** 48–54
Chesapeake Bay **4:** 13; **6:** 19; **7:** 16; **10:** 10, 12–13, 15
Church, Benjamin **2:** 12, 18
Cincinnatus **2:** 44–45
Clark, George Rogers **8:** 11–16

Clinton, George **10:** 39
Clinton, Henry **2:** 55, 63, 66; **3:** 10–11, *54–55*, 59; **4:** 48; **5:** 55–58; **7:** 40–41, 43–44, 47–52, 55–56, 65; **8:** 34–37, 48–54, 61; **9:** 11, 14, 24, 31, 44, *65*; **10:** 6, 8, 10, 12–13, 21, 24, *66*
Clinton, James **8:** *24–25*
Clymer, George **3:** 60
Colonies, life in **1:** 8–16
Committees of Correspondence **1:** 44, 53, 57
Communication: **4:** 10; **5:** 9–10, 56; **6:** 16
Concord (Mass.), battle **2:** 16, 18–19, 21, 28–44
Congress, United States **10:** *24*, 26–28, 31–32, 34–35, 38, 45, 49
Connecticut **2:** 6–7, 50; **6:** 13; **8:** 65–66; **10:** 6
Constitution, United States **10:** 39–40, 58, 61
Continental Army **2:** 51–52; **3:** *11–12*, 13, 36, 63–66; **4:** 44–45; **6:** 24–25, 46–50, 52–56; **7:** 36, 45, 47; **8:** 19, 25, 42, 47, 52; **9:** 34–35, 37, 39, 50, 58–60; **10:** 6–8, *14*, 26, *30*, 32, 37, 40, 54, 57
    Dragoons **9:** 29, 35
    Light infantry **5:** 51, 61; **6:** 25; **8:** 37; **10:** 18
    Ranks/Officers **3:** 12–16; **6:** 14; **10:** 34, 68
    Strength **3:** 13, 25–26, 31, 36, 40; **4:** 15, 22, 31, 38–39, 42–43, 47, 52, 58; **5:** 11, 21, 31, 40, 44, 58, 64; **6:** 11, 24, 36; **7:** 47, 60, 66–67; **8:** 24, 28, 30, 47, 51, 57, 65; **9:** 27, 30, 35, 47, 58, 65; **10:** 12–13, 16
Continental Congress
    First **1:** 6–7, 58–60
    Second **2:** 46–47, 51–52; **3:** 11–13, 24, 36, 40, 55, 62, 65–66; **4:** 15, 22, 29–30, 32, 44–46, 49–50; **5:** 11, 13, 17–18, 28, 38, 45, 65, 67; **6:** 8, 10, 14–16, 20–21, 29, 34–35, 42–44, 51–52, 61, 66–67; **7:** 13, 15–16, 18, 20, 31, 47, 59, 61, 66; **8:** 17, 23, 40, 55, 65–67; **9:** 10, 26–27; **10:** 8–9, 38, 40, 55
Continental Marines **3:** 13; **6:** 37; **7:** 15–16, 24, 30; **8:** 40
Continental Navy **7:** 11–20, 32, 36; **8:** 40
    Ranks **10:** 68
Conway Cabal **6:** 42–44, 52
Conway, Thomas **6:** 43–44
Cornwallis, Charles **4:** 48–50, 58–59, 61; **5:** 9; **6:** 9, 23, 25, 27, 35, 58; **7:** 44, 52; **8:** 48–49, 54–56, 59; **9:** 16, *18*, 24–25, 27–31, 42, 44–52, 54, 56–58; **10:** 12, 15–16, 18–19, 22,

26, 28, *66*
Cowpens (S.C.), battle **9:** 32–44, 46; **10:** *57*
Cruger, John **9:** 64
Cunningham, Patrick **3:** 53
Currency, Continental **3:** 65–66; **6:** 14, 50;
   8: 42–43, 47, 67; **9:** 10; **10:** *9*

Davie, William **8:** *62;* **9:** 60
Davis, Isaac **2:** 32, 34
Dawes, William **2:** 24–25, 28
Deane, Silas **5:** 13; **6:** *20,* 61
Dearborn, Henry **2:** 58; **5:** *51,* 61; **8:** 24
Declaration of Independence **1:** 7; **3:** 60–63;
   7: 40; **10:** 39, 44–45
Delaplace, William **2:** 50–*51*
Delaware **1:** 19; **2:** 6; **6:** 17, 19, 34, 53
Delaware River **4:** 28, 49–50, 53–58; **6:** 17, 19,
   35–36, 41–43; **7:** 43–44, 48; **10:** *57*
Desertion **3:** 32; **4:** 15; **5:** 31, 58; **6:** 33; **7:** 9;
   8: 65; **9:** 47, 56, 65, 67–68
Disease **3:** 35, 40; **4:** 15–16, 22, 41; **6:** 33, 49;
   7: 9, 38, 65; **8:** 17, 29–30, 57, 67; **9:** 49, 63
Drill; see Training, military
Duportail, Louis **6:** *17*

East India Company **1:** 50, 53
England **1:** 46–47, 53, 57; **3:** 9; **4:** 44, 51;
   5: 11–13; **6:** 62–63, 66; **7:** 21–23, 32–33, 35,
   38–39; **8:** 6, 31–33, 50; **9:** 57; **10:** 31–32, 36,
   43, 47–48, 53
d'Estaing, Charles **7:** 39, 47, 58–61, 68;
   8: 28–31; **9:** 6
Europe **1:** 8, 14, 24–25, 35, 37; **3:** 19; **6:** 35;
   7: 21, 31; **10:** 25, 36
Eutaw Springs (S.C.), battle **9:** 65–68

Fanning, David **9:** 64
Farm, Matthias **5:** 22
Farnsworth, Amos **2:** 65
Ferguson, Patrick **9:** 18–25
Flag, United States **6:** *10,* 22; **10:** 43
Fletchall, Thomas **3:** 53
Florida **7:** 65–66; **8:** 31–32; **10:** 53
Fort Anne **5:** 23–24
Fort Duquesne **1:** 22, 24
Fort Edward **5:** 28–29
Fort Granby **9:** 63
Fort Johnson **3:** 55; **8:** 50, 52

Fort Johnston **3:** 49–50
Fort Lee **4:** 42–43, 47
Fort Mercer **6:** 41–42
Fort Mifflin **6:** 41–42
Fort Motte **9:** 63
Fort Moultrie **3:** 55–59; **7:** 63; **8:** 31, 50, 52–53
Fort Necessity **1:** *22–23,* 24
Fort Sackville **8:** 15–16
Fort Stanwix **5:** 11, 14, 40–45; **6:** 9
Fort Ticonderoga **1:** 34; **2:** 7, 50–51; **3:** 23–24,
   28, 38; **4:** 16–17, 20; **5:** 11, 14, 16, 20–22,
   24–25, 30, 45–46, 55; **6:** 9, 16
Fort Washington **4:** 38, 40, 42–43, 47
Fort Watson **9:** 59
Fort William and Mary **2:** 10–11
Fox, Charles **3:** 8–9; **10:** 23
France **4:** 63; **5:** 1–13, 65; **6:** 41, 60–67; **7:** 8,
   20, 23, 32–33, 35, 38–39, 59; **8:** 6, 31, 55,
   67; **9:** 10; **10:** 25, 31, 36, 57–58, 61, 63–64
Francisco, Peter **9:** *56*
Franklin, Benjamin **1:** 16, 28, 36, 39, 41, 53;
   2: 46, *50;* **3:** 60, 62; **4:** 29–*30,* 51; **6:** 61–66;
   7: 26; **8:** 32; **10:** 31, *41,* 52–53, *61*
Fraser, Simon **5:** 24–25, 50, 53, 55, 61–*63*
Freeman's Farm (Saratoga), battle **5:** 50–55, 58
French alliance **6:** 41, 60–67; **7:** 32, 41, 47, 61,
   68; **8:** 13, 32; **9:** 6
French and Indian War **1:** 17–37; **2:** 7, 11, *51,*
   59; **3:** 24; **5:** 2, 17; **8:** 6
French armed forces **1:** 22–26, 31, 34–35;
   8: 29–31; **9:** 6, *9;* **10:** 13, 16, 19, *58*
   Engineers **10:** 16, 19
French fleet **7:** 33–34, 38–39, 47, 59–60;
   8: 28–29, 32; **9:** 6, 10; **10:** 10–11, 13, 15–16,
   25
Frontier **1:** 29; **8:** 6–7; **9:** 19; **10:** 42, 48, 50

Gage, Thomas **1:** 28–29, 40, 54, *61–63;*
   2: *10–12,* 18–19, 21–22, 26, 44–45, 50,
   55–57; **3:** 10–11, 37
Galloway, Joseph **6:** 60; **7:** 44
Gansevoort, Peter **5:** 40
Gaspee incident **1:** *47–49*
Gates, Horatio **1:** 29; **3:** 12, *15;* **4:** 16, 18, 52;
   5: 45, 48, 50–51, 53, 55, 58, 60, 64; **6:** 43;
   8: 55, 57, 59–60, 65, 67; **9:** 10, 16, 26; **10:** *61*
George II, King **1:** 16, 22; **3:** 50
George III, King **1:** 16, 41, 42, 45, 46, 48, 55,

60–63; **2**: 11, 44, 52; **3**: 6, 9; **4**: 12, 29, 63; **5**: 6–7, 14, 25; **7**: 62, 68; **8**: 32, 61; **9**: 57; **10**: 22–23, 49, *67*

Georgia **1**: 12, 58, 60; **7**: 43, 65–68; **8**: 27–29, 36, *55–56*, 61, 65; **9**: 16, 30, 44, 58, 63; **10**: 45, 61
   Savannah **1**: 12; **7**: 65–66; **8**: 27, 29–31, 48, 56, 61; **9**: 6, 68; **10**: 25

Germain, George **3**: *6–8*, 37; **4**: 10, 14; **5**: 6–8, 11, 14; **7**: 41; **8**: 48; **9**: 31; **10**: 22

German Battalion **4**: 52, 58

Germantown (Pa.), battle **6**: 36–41, 63

Girty, Simon **8**: 11, 16

Glover, John **4**: 28, 38, 53, 66

Government, United States **10**: 38–40
   Political parties **10**: 39, 42

de Grasse, Francois **8**: *29*; **10**: 10, 13, *15*, 25

Graves, Thomas **10**: 13, *15*, 21

Great Bridge (Va.), battle **3**: 49

Great Britain; see British; also see England

Green Mountain Boys **2**: 50–51; **3**: 28; **5**: 24

Greene, Christopher **7**: 36

Greene, Nathanael **2**: 54; **4**: 24, 31–32, 43; **6**: 20–21, *24*, 28, 52; **7**: 50, 55.59; **8**: 47, 55; **9**: 25–32, 44, 46–47, 49–52, 55–60, 62–65, *67–68*; **10**: 9, 12, 25, 57, *61*

Grey, Charles **6**: 31–32

Grierson, Benjamin **9**: 63

Guerillas; see also Partisans **4**: 8; **8**: 62; **9**: 16, 29, 35

Guilford Courthouse (N.C.), battle **9**: 49–58, 62; **10**: 12, 57

Hale, Nathan **4**: 40; **9**: *15*

Hamilton, Alexander **4**: *56*, 61, 66; **6**: 53; **8**: 59; **10**: 18, *39*, 45, 62

Hamilton, Henry **8**: 9, 14–15

Hancock, John **2**: 6–7, 19, 24–25, 46; **3**: 60

Hand, Edward **4**: 58, 66; **8**: 23

Harlem Heights (N.Y.), battle **4**: 32, *34–35*, *36*, 38

Hart, Nancy **8**: 64

Hausegger, Nicholas **4**: *52*, 58

Heath, William **4**: 42; **10**: 13

Henry, Patrick **1**: *38–39*, 40, 44, 59; **3**: 11, *46–48*; **8**: 11, 14; **10**: 39, *62*

Herkimer, Nicholas **5**: 41–*42*

Hessians **4**: 12–15, 48–49, 52, 53, 55–57, 63;

5: *11*, 14, 20, 23, 25, 29, *33–35*, 61; **6**: 24, 26, 30, 41–42, 58; **7**: 37, 40, 48, 52; **8**: 46; **10**: *57*

Hobkirk's Hill (S.C.), battle **9**: 59–60, 62

Hopkins, Esek **7**: *13*, 15–16

Horses; see also Cavalry **3**: *20*, 22; **4**: 9–10; **5**: 29, 58; **6**: 19; **8**: 49, 53

Howard, John **9**: 34, 39, 42

Howe, Richard **4**: 21, 29–*30*; **6**: 19; **7**: 35, 40, 43, 58–60; **10**: *67*

Howe, Robert **7**: 65–66

Howe, William **2**: 55, 60–61, 63; **3**: 10–11, 37, 42, 44; **4**: 6, 11, 14, 21–22, 25, 27, 29, 36, 38–40, 42–43, 62–63, 66; **5**: 6–7, 9–11, 26, 56; **6**: 9–13, 16–19, 22, 25, 28–31, 33, 35–36, 41, 56–57, 60; **10**: *67*

Hubbardton (N.Y.), battle **5**: 24–25, 32

Huddy, Joshua **10**: 24

Hudson Highlands **4**: 42; **5**: 11, 48, 55–57; **6**: 8; **8**: 37; **9**: 11–12, 14

Hudson River **4**: 21–24, 40, 42–43, 52, 63; **5**: 7, 10–11, 16, 27–29, 40, 45–48, 51, 55, 57–59; **6**: 8, 12, 16; **8**: 37, 39; **9**: 11; **10**: 10

Huger, Isaac **9**: 59–60

Hutchinson, Thomas **1**: 40

Illinois
   Kaskaskia **8**: 13

Indians; see Native Americans

Indiana
   Vincennes **8**: 13–15

Ireland **3**: 54; **4**: 12; **7**: 33

Iroquois; see also Native Americans **5**: 17; **8**: 16–18, 23, 25–26; **10**: 49–50

Jasper, William **3**: *58–59*; **8**: 31

Jay, John **4**: 32; **10**: 31, 39, *44–45*

Jefferson, Thomas **1**: 44; **2**: 46; **3**: 61–62; **9**: 27; **10**: 34–35

Johnson, Guy **8**: 18

Johnson, William **8**: 18

Jones, David **5**: 32

Jones, John Paul **7**: *20–22*, 24, 26–27, 30–32; **10**: *41*

de Kalb **6**: *20–21*; **8**: 55, *59–60*

Kaskaskia (Ill.) **8**: 13

Kettle Creek (Ga.), battle **7**: 67–68

Kentucky **8:** 7–8, 11, 13, 15–16; **10:** 42–43
King's Mountain (S.C.), battle **9:** 20–24
Knowlton, Thomas **2:** 58, 60–61, 66; **4:** 34
Knox, Henry **3:** 23, 37–41; **4:** 53, 66; **6:** *19–20*, 22; **7:** *55*; **10:** 39, 50, *63*
Knyphausen, Wilhelm **6:** 23, 25, 27; **7:** 44, 52; **8:** 49
Kosciuszko, Thaddeus **5:** 20, *48*; **6:** 21

Lafayette, Marquis de **6:** *20–22*, 28; **7:** 36, 47, 50, 59; **8:** 19, 66; **9:** 27; **10:** 11–12, 18, 57, *63*
Lake Champlain; see also Valcour Island **1:** 31, 34; **2:** 50; **4:** 16–21; **5:** 14, 20–21, 23
Lake George **1:** *30–31*, 34; **5:** 28–29
Landais, Pierre **7:** 30
Langdon, John **2:** 11
Laurens, Henry **6:** *34*; **10:** 31
Learned, Ebenezer **5:** 61
Lee, Arthur **6:** 61
Lee, Charles **3:** 12, 15, *55–56*; **4:** 40–41, 46–50, 52; **7:** 46–48, 50–52, 54, 56–57
Lee, Henry **6:** 53; **8:** *39–40*; **9:** 27, 29–30, *48–49*, 59, 63–64, 68
Lee, Richard Henry **3:** 62; **6:** 43; **10:** *38–39*
Lee, William **7:** 36
Leslie, Thomas **2:** 12–13, *14*, 17
Lewis, Francis **3:** 61
Lexington (Mass.), battle **2:** 16, 18–19, 24–44
Lillington, Alexander **3:** 51
Lincoln, Benjamin **5:** 26, *32–33*, 48, 58, 60; **7:** 66–68; **8:** 28, 30–31, 50–53, 65; **10:** 9
Livingston, Robert **3:** 62
London **1:** *14–15*, 41
Long, Pierce **5:** 23
Long Island (N.Y.), campaign **4:** 22–29; **5:** 13
Louis XVI, King **6:** 63–65
Lovell, Solomon **8:** 41
Loyalists **1:** 7, 62–63; **2:** 6, 52; **3:** 44, 48, 51, 53, 59, 64; **4:** 29, 50, 55; **5:** 9–10, 16–17, 30, 33, 45, 56, 58, 60; **6:** 10–11, 13, 26–27, 34–35, 60; **7:** 40, 43–44, 48, 62–63, 66–68; **8:** 12, 18–19, 22, 25, 52, 60–62, 64; **9:** 16, 18, 23–24, 35, 48–49, 58–59, 62–64, 67; **10:** 24–25, 32–33, 48, 51–54, 57, 61

MacArthur, Archibald **9:** 42
Madison, James **10:** 39, *63*
Maine **3:** 26, 30–31; **8:** 40–42

Maham, Hezekiah **9:** *59*
Marblehead Regiment **4:** 27–28, 38, 53
Marion, Francis **8:** 31; **9:** 29–31, 58–59, *61*, 63, *68*
Marshall, John **3:** 48; **8:** 59
Martin, Joseph **8:** 47
Martin, Josiah **3:** 49–50, 55
Maryland **1:** 12; **2:** 6, 51; **4:** 46, 49; **9:** 27; **10:** 33, 35
Massachusetts **1:** 54–56, 59–60; **2:** 6, 11, 18, 55; **7:** 18; **8:** 40
    Boston **1:** 9, 41–45, 52–55, 57, 62–63; **2:** 12–13, 18–19, 22–23, 42, 45, 51, 53–55; **3:** 10, 15, 23, 36–45; **8:** 40
    Cambridge **2:** 20, 22; **3:** 12–13, 26
    Committee of Safety **2:** 6, 12, 18–20, 45, 55
    Provincial Congress **2:** 6, 18, 47, 50; **3:** 11; **5:** 17
    Salem **2:** 12–13, *14–15*, 16–17
Maxwell, William **6:** 25; **8:** 23
McCrea, Jane **5:** 31–33, 45, 58
McHenry, James **10:** 39
McLane, Allan **6:** *59*
Medicine **2:** 42–43; **8:** 65, 67
Mercenaries, German; see Hessians
Mercer, Hugh **4:** 56, 59–61
Michigan
    Detroit **8:** 9, 15
Mifflin, Thomas **4:** *52*; **6:** 43; **7:** 47
Military discipline **2:** 48–49; **3:** 15, 19; **4:** 44; **6:** 25, 55, 59; **8:** 25, 65–66; **9:** 27–28; **10:** 8
Military planning
    American **3:** 41; **4:** 34–35, 53, 58; **5:** 11, 55; **6:** 5, 36–37; **7:** 50; **8:** 23, 52; **9:** 30–32, 34, 58, 62; **10:** 10
    British **4:** 12–14, 21; **5:** 7, 9–11, 14, 26, 57; **6:** 9–11, 16, 23; **7:** 33–35, 38, 43, 59, 61–65, 68; **8:** 52, 54; **9:** 31, 44; **10:** 12
Militia; see also Minutemen **1:** 19, 22, 25, 60; **2:** 6–7, 10, 12, 16–18, 21–22, 26, 28–29, 53–54, 63, 66; **3:** 13, 36, 47–49, 51–53, 66; **4:** 33, 39–40, 43, 45, 48; **5:** 26, 30, 32–33, 36, 41, 45, 48, 58; **6:** 14, 19, 24–25; **7:** 36–37, 59, 63, 67–68; **8:** 13–15, 19, 28, 41, 50, 55, 57, 59; **9:** 10, 18–19, 32, 34–35, 38–40, 42, 47–48, 51; **10:** 16, 39–40, 51, 57
Minutemen; see also Militia **2:** 6, 17, 24–28, 32, 35; **5:** 17

Mississippi River   **1:** 21; **8:** 11–14, 31; **10:** 32, 38, 50

Mohawk Valley   **5:** 14, 18, 40, 44, 46; **6:** 9; **8:** 23–24

Monck's Corner (S.C.), battle   **8:** 52–53

Monckton, Henry   **7:** 55

Monmouth Court House (N.J.), battle **7:** 50–57; **8:** 19

Monongahela River   **1:** 22, 29; **2:** 11

Monroe, James   **4:** *56–57*

Montgomery, Richard   **3:** 12, 25–26, 28–35, 37; **4:** 15

Moore's Creek (N.C.), battle   **3:** 50–53, 55

Morale   **3:** 59; **4:** 31, 35, 43, 63; **5:** 31, 66; **6:** 11, 33; **8:** 39–40, 55

Morgan, Daniel   **1:** 29; **3:** 18, 26, 34–*35;* **5:** 26, 51–52, 60–61; **8:** 19, 24; **9:** 30–32, 34–35, 38–39, 42, 44, 46, 49–50; **10:** 57, *64*

Morris, Gouverneur   **10:** 39

Morris, Robert   **10:** *8–9,* 39

Moultrie, William   **3:** 56

Munroe, William   **2:** 25–26

Murray, John, Earl of Dunmore   **3:** 46–49

Muskets; see Weapons

Mutiny   **8:** 65–66; **10:** 6–8

Native Americans; see also Iroquois; Oneidas **1:** 18, *19–23,* 25, *26–27,* 29, 31, *32–33,* 37, 59; **2:** 51, 53; **5:** *17–19,* 20, 23, 30–32, 40–42, 45, 48; **7:** 65; **8:** 6–11, 14–26; **9:** 19, 34; **10:** 43, 48–50

Negroes; see African Americans

New England   **1:** 56; **2:** 18, 51; **3:** 11–12, 46; **4:** 13, 47, 63; **5:** 7, 26, 28, 32, 43; **7:** : 13, 63; **8:** 40; **10:** 8

New France; see also Canada   **1:** 20–21, 31

New Hampshire   **2:** 6, 10–11, 54; **5:** 13–17, 30, 33

New Jersey   **4:** 42, 47–50, 53, 62; **5:** 9; **6:** 8–12, 36, 41, 50; **7:** 43–44, 49, 51–57; **8:** 48; **10:** 8, 24

   Morristown   **4:** 61; **5:** 6, 11; **6:** 8, 11; **8:** *44–45,* 47, 65; **9:** 8; **10:** 57

   Princeton   **4:** 54, 58–61

   Trenton   **4:** *53–58,* 61

New York   **1:** 9;31, 34, 40–41, 50–51, 53, 57, 60; **2:** 43, 47, 51; **3:** 40, 59; **4:** 18–19, 21–43, 62–64; **5:** 6–7, 9–11, 14–18, 20–32, 40–46,

48–67; **6:** 8, 10, 16, 66; **7:** 37, 41, 43, 56–59, 61, 65; **8:** 16–26, 34–35, 37, 39, 42, 48–49; **9:** 6, 8, 10–11; **10:** 6, 8, 10, 12–13, 25–26

   Albany   **5:** 14, 16, 26–27, 29, 46–48, 57

   Burning of   **4:** 36–37

   Manhattan   **4:** 31–33, 38

   Oswego   **5:** 18, 40

   West Point   **5:** 57; **9:** 8, 11–14

Newburgh (N.Y.) Addresses   **10:** 29–31

Ninety–Six (S.C.), siege   **9:** 64–65

North, Frederick   **1:** 48–49; **2:** 18; **3:** 6, *8–9;* **4:** 63; **5:** 6; **6:** 66–67; **7:** 62; **10:** 22–23, 31

North Carolina   **3:** 49–53; **8:** 60–63, 65; **9:** 16, 18, 24, 27, 44, 47, 58, 68; **10:** 12

O'Hara, Charles   **9:** 45; **10:** 22

Ohio   **10:** 43, 46, 48–49

Ohio Company   **1:** 22

Ohio River   **1:** 22, 56; **8:** 7–8, 11

Old World; see also Europe   **1:** 8, 18

Olive Branch Petition   **2:** 52

Oneidas; see also Native Americans   **5:** 18; **8:** 17–19; **10:** 50

Oriskany (N.Y.), battle   **5:** 41–43, 45

Otis, James   **1:** 41

Over–Mountain Men   **9:** 19–24

Paine, Thomas   **4:** 50–52; **10:** *64*

Paoli (Pa.), battle   **6:** 31–33

Parker, John   **2:** 27–29

Parker, Jonas   **2:** 28

Parker, Peter   **3:** 55, 59

Parliament   **1:** 15, 37–39, 41–42, 45, 50, 54–55, 60; **2:** 18–19; **3:** 8–9; **6:** 66; **10:** 22–23

Partisans; see also Guerillas   **8:** 62, 64; **9:** 29–30, 58–61, 64

Paulus Hook (N.J.), battle   **8:** 39–40, 42

Peace conference, 1776   **4:** 29–30

Peace treaty; see Treaty of Paris

Pearson, Richard   **7:** 26

Penn, Richard   **2:** 52

Pennsylvania   **1:** 22, 29; **2:** 51; **4:** 52; **6:** 23–28, 41, 43, 50; **7:** 43; **8:** 7, 16, 19–21, 23–24; **9:** 12, 27; **10:** 7–8

   Philadelphia   **1:** 6–7, 9, *10–11, 12–13,* 50–51, 53, 57–58, *59;* **2:** 43, *46–47;* **4:** 49; **5:** 10, 26; **6:** 8, 11, 14, 17, 19, 29–31, 33–35, 42, 50, 56–60, 66; **7:** 20, 40–41, 43–44,

47–48, 68; **8:** 48; **9:** 6, 12; **10:** 8, 39, 65

Valley Forge **6:** 45–57, 60; **7:** 45–47, 52, *56;* **8:** 19, 47, 65–66; **10:** 57

Wyoming Valley **8:** 19, *20–21*

Penobscot Bay (Maine), battle **8:** 40–42

Pepperell, William **1:** 18

Percy, Hugh **2:** 36–38, 44

Phillips, William **5:** 21; **10:** 11–12

Pickens, Andrew **7:** *67–68;* **9:** 34, 38, 42, 58, 63

Pickering, Timothy **2:** 12, *16;* **10:** 9, 39

Pigot, Robert **2:** 61, 63

Pitcairn, John **2:** 26–29, 63, 65

"Pitcher," Molly **7:** *57*

Pollard, Asa **2:** *57*

Pomeroy, Seth **2:** *59*

Pontiac's War **1:** 37

Poor, Enoch **5:** 60; **8:** 24

Poor, Salem **7:** 36

Population **1:** 9, 11, 14; **3:** 64; **6:** 67; **7:** 63; **8:** 17; **10:** 46–47, 53

Prescott, William **2:** *57–58,* 66

Prevost, Augustine **7:** 65, 67; **8:** 27–29

Princeton (N.J.), battle **4:** *58–61, 64–65;* **5:** 7, 10, 13; **6:** 6–7; **7:** 55

Prisoners **3:** 60; **4:** 41, 43; **5:** 38, 48, 64–65; **6:** 35; **7:** 23, 31, 67–68; **9:** 24; **10:** 24–25

Privateers **7:** 17–19; **8:** 40

Propaganda **2:** 43

Pulaski, Casimir **6:** *21;* **8:** *31*

Putnam, Israel **1:** 29; **2:** *45, 59,* 61, 66; **3:** 15; **4:** 24–25, 32–33

Pyle, John **9:** 48

Quakers **1:** 12; **6:** 34; **9:** 26; **10:** 44

Quebec, see Canada

Quincy, Josiah **1:** 44

Rall, Johann **4:** 53, *55–56*

Ranger **7:** 20, *22–23, 33*

Rations; see Supplies, military

Rawdon, Francis **9:** 59–60, 62–65

Recruiting **4:** 12, 44–45, 58; **6:** 6, 8; **7:** 9, 17, 19; **8:** 66; **9:** 27

Redcoats; see British armed forces

Reed, Joseph **4:** 34; **9:** 27

"Regulators" **1:** 49; **3:** 50–51, 55

Revere, Paul **1:** 53, 57, 59; **2:** 10, 16, *18–26,* 28; **8:** 41

Rhode Island **1:** 19, 41, 47; **2:** 6, 54; **6:** 28; **7:** 41, 56–57, 60–61; **8:** 50; **9:** 6, 26

Newport **1:** 9; **4:** 48, 64; **5:** 7; **6:** 10; **7:** 59–61; **8:** 28, 30–31, 49; **9:** 6, 9–10; **10:** 9, 11

Richardson, Richard **3:** 53

Riedesel, Friedrich **5:** *20,* 23, 25, 29–30, 51, 54

Riedesel, Baroness Friederika **8:** 46

Rifles; see Weapons

Robertson, James **8:** 61

Rochambeau, Jean **9:** 6, 9–10; **10:** 9–10, 13, 18, 58, *64*

Rockingham, Charles **3:** 8–9

Ross, Elizabeth (Betsy) **6:** 10

Royal governors **1:** 14–15, 22, 44, 49, 51, 53–54; **2:** 11; **3:** 46–47, 49–50, 55; **5:** 7; **8:** 61

Royal Navy **1:** 29, 38, 47; **2:** 57; **3:** 54–56, 59; **4:** 6, 12, 18, 25, 27, 39, 65–66; **5:** 58; **6:** 17, 66; **7:** 6–11, 17, 20, 32–33, 60–61, 63, 65; **8:** 28, 32–33, 42, 52, 54; **9:** 8, 11, 58; **10:** 11–13, 15

Ruggles, Timothy **1:** 63

Rules of war **8:** 61–62; **9:** 14–15; **10:** 52

Quarter **8:** 53–54; **9:** 24

Rush, Benjamin **6:** *43–44;* **10:** 44

Rutledge, Edward **4:** 29–*30*

Rutledge, John **3:** 56; **8:** 50

Saltonstall, Dudley **8:** 40–42

Sandwich, John **7:** 6, 33, 35

St. Clair, Arthur **5:** *20–21,* 24–25

St. Lawrence River **1:** 31, 35; **3:** 31–32; **4:** 15; **5:** 14

St. Leger, Barry **5:** 14, 18, *40–42,* 45

Saratoga (N.Y.), battles **5:** 48–67; **6:** 41, 43, 63; **7:** 68; **8:** 17; **9:** 11; **10:** 57

Savannah (Ga.), siege **8:** 29–31

Scammell, Alexander **10:** 16

Schuyler, Philip **3:** 24–26; **5:** 26–29, 31, 43–45; **8:** 17

Settlers

British **1:** 18–19, 21, 29, 33; **5:** 17; **8:** 6, 8

French **1:** 20–21, 29; **8:** 6

Seven Years' War **1:** 35; **3:** 6; **7:** 39, 41

Sevier, John **9:** 19

Shelburne, William **10:** 31

Sherman, Roger **3:** 61–62

Ships **1:** 9, 47; **4:** 8–10, 17–19, 22, 65–66;

7: 6–19, 26, 39, 60, 62; 8: 29, 32, 42–43, 49; 10: 21

Skenesboro (N.Y.), battle 5: 21, 23–25

Slave trade 1: *13*; 10: 44–45

Slavery 1: 12–13; 7: 37; 10: 44–47, 63

Smallwood, William 9: *26*

Smith, Francis 2: 21–23, 35–36

Smith, Jeremiah 1: 33

Smuggling 1: 38, 47, 52

Sons of Liberty 1: 41–42, 44, 53, 63

South Carolina 3: 53; 4: 13; 8: 61, 63, 65; 9: 16, 30–32, 44, 58–59, 62–63, 65; 10: 12, 45, 50

Charleston 1: 12, 41, 53; 2: 43; 3: 46, 54–59; 7: 63, 66; 8: 28, 31, 48–54, 56–57, 62; 9: 68; 10: 25, 52

Spain 5: 13; 6: 65; 7: 33, 38; 8: 31–34; 10: 36, 38

Spies 2: 12, 18–20, 23, 55; 4: 40, 59; 5: 13, 23; 7: 36; 9: 12, 14–15

Stark, John 2: 58, 61; 5: 30, 32–36, 38, 64

Starvation 3: 31, 64–66; 4: 41; 5: 58; 6: 48–49; 8: 47, 65–66; 9: 9; 10: 8

State troops 6: 37; 9: 35

Stephen, Adam 6: 24, 27

Steuben, Friedrich 6: 21, 53–55; 7: 47, 55–56; 8: 47; 9: 15, 27; 10: 57, *65*

Stevens, Edward 9: 47, 50

Stewart, Alexander 9: 64, 67

Stony Point, (N.Y.), battle 8: 37–39

Strategy; see Military planning

Submarine *Turtle* 4: 37–38

Sullivan, John 2: *10–11*; 4: 16–17, 24, 29, 52; 6: 20, 24–25, 27; 7: 59–60; 8: 23–26, 30; 10: 49

Sumter, Thomas 8: 62, 64; 9: 58–59, 63–64

Supplies, military 2: 7, 12; 3: 31, 40, 44, 63–66; 4: 6–9, 11, 16–17; 5: 13, 16, 29–30, 46, 48, 56; 6: 14, 30, 42, 45, 48–53, 62; 7: 44–45, *67*; 8: 42–43, 47, 57, 65–67; 9: 9, 27, 44–45, 58; 10: 6, 8, 26, 29

Tactics, see Military Planning

Tarleton, Banastre 8: 52, *53*–54, 59, 62, 64; 9: 24, 31–32, 34–36, 38–*39*, 42–44, 48; 10: 67

Taxes 1: 36–42, 47, 50; 3: 9; 6: 66; 10: 40

Tennessee 10: 42–43

Thayendanegea; see Brant, Joseph

Thomson, William 3: 53

Tilghman, Tench 6: 22; 10: 28

Tories; see Loyalists

Trade 1: 11–12, 14, 37–38, 42, 47–50, 57; 2: 14, 18; 3: 63–64; 7: 38, 63–64; 8: 17, 28; 10: 36, 38

Training, military 2: 48–49; 6: 53–55; 7: 47, 52

Trappers 2: 21, 22; 8: 6

Treaty of Paris 10: 31–32, 47–49

Trenton (N.J.), battle 4: 53–57; 5: 7, 10, 13; 6: 6–7

Trumbull, John 2: 17, 53; 5: 20

Tryon, William 1: 49, 51

Turner, Nat 10: 46

Uniforms 1: 26, *36–37*; 2: 6–7, *17, 19*; 3: *9, 11, 14, 17–18, 20*; 4: *10, 13, 22, 48, 53*; 5: *11, 24–25, 33*; 6: *9, 22, 25–26, 37*; 7: : *61*; 8: *43, 47*; 9: *34, 36–37*; 10: *14*

Valcour Island 4: 17–21

Vergennes, Charles 5: 12–13; 6: 62–64; 8: 32

Vermont 2: 50; 5: 30, 32–39, 48

Veterans 10: 42–43, *57*

Vincennes (Ind.) 8: 13–15

Virginia 1: 8, 12, *19*, 22, 29, 33, 40, 44, 56, 58; 2: 6, 51–52; 3: 11–12, 46–49; 8: 11, 15; 9: 18, 27, 31; 10: 10–13, 46, 61–62

Mount Vernon 1: 20–21; 3: 12; 10: *15*, 65

Norfolk 3: 46–49

Riflemen, Virginia 3: 18, 26, 34–35; 5: 51–52; 9: *34*

Yorktown 10: 12, 16

Virginia Capes, battle 10: 13, 15

Walton, George 3: 61

War of 1812 10: 47–48, 50, 63

Ward, Artemas 2: 53, 55, 58; 3: 15, 38

Warner, Seth 3: 28; 5: 24–25, 32, 35

Warren, Joseph 2: 47, 59–60, 65

Washington, D.C. 10: 65

Washington, George 1: 20–25, 28–29; 2: 46–47, 52; 3: 11–*12*, 13–15, 26, 36, 38, 40–41, 44, 66; 4: 22–28, 31–40, 42–50, 52–53, 55–63; 5: 6, 10–11, 26, 33; 6: 6–9, *11*–16, 19, 21, 24–25, 27–29, 36–38, 40–44, *46*–48, *51*–55, 63–67; 7: 11, 36, 41, 45–52, 54–59, 61, 68;

8: 19, 23, 26, 37–39, 42–43, 46–47, 55, 65–67; **9:** 8–10, 14–15, 26–28; **10:** 6, 8–13, 16, 18, 24–29, 31, 33, 35, 38–42, 52, 54–55, 57–58, 65

Washington, Martha **6:** 57; **10:** 65

Washington, William **4:** 56, 66; **9:** 35, 39–41, 43, 54

Wayne, Anthony **6:** 24, 30, 31–32, 38–40, 53; **7:** 50, 55; **8:** 36–39; **10:** 8, 12, 25

Waxhaws (S.C.), battle **8:** 54–55; **9:** 24, 41

Weapons
 Bayonets **2:** 49, 62, 65; **6:** 31; **9:** 38
 Cannons/Artillery pieces **2:** 16; **3:** 22–23; **4:** 53; **5:** 21, 57, 60; **7:** 7, 26, 49; **10:** 58
 Gunpowder **4:** 66
 Muskets **2:** 48–49; **3:** 16–18; **7:** 12; **9:** 27
 Pistols **3:** 21
 Rifles **3:** 17–18
 Sabers/Swords **3:** 21

West Indies **1:** 9, 37, 57; **2:** 18; **3:** 63; **4:** 66; **7:** 16, 37–38, 43, 64; **8:** 28–29, 31, 33–34; **9:** 6, 10; **10:** 25–26, 36, 53

Whipple, Abraham **1:** 48–49; **8:** 50, 52

Whipple, Prince **4:** 55

White, Philip **10:** 24

White Plains (N.Y.), battle **4:** 39–40

Wilderness **1:** 21, 28, 31; **8:** 8

Wilkes, John **3:** 8

Wilkinson, James **5:** 53, 60, 62

Willett, Marinus **5:** 42

Williams, Otho Holland **9:** 47

Winter quarters **4:** 50, 61; **5:** 6, 11; **6:** 8, 45–60; **8:** 14, 42–45, 47, 65; **9:** 8–9; **10:** 6, 8, 29

Wolfe, James **1:** 35

Women
 Acland, Lady Harriet **5:** 61
 Adams, Abigail **10:** 60
 Arnold, Peggy (Shippen) **7:** 48; **10:** 60
 Hart, Nancy **8:** 64
 McCrea, Jane **5:** 31–33, 45, 58
 "Molly Pitcher" **7:** 57
 Mrs. Motte **9:** 62–63
 Mrs. Murray story **4:** 33
 Riedesel, Baroness Friederika **8:** 46
 Ross, Elizabeth (Betsy) **6:** 10
 Traveling with armies **4:** 9–10; **5:** 20, 61; **8:** 46
 Washington, Martha **6:** 57; **10:** 65

Woodford, William **3:** 48–49

Wooster, David **6:** 13

Wyoming (Pa.) "Massacre" **8:** 19–21

Yorktown (Va.), Siege **10:** 16–23, 58

Yost, Hon **5:** 45

Acknowledgments

Author's collection: 8B, 9B, 46

Eldridge S. Brooks, *The Century Book of the American Revolution*, 1897: 51

Anne S. K. Brown Military Collection, John Hay Library, Brown University, Providence, Rhode Island: 42–43, 53, 55, 61

J. G. Heck. *Iconographic Encyclopedia of Science, Literature, and Art*, 1851: 8–9, 60

Independence National Historical Park: 20, 50B, 66

Library of Congress: 13, 44–45, 49, 56, 58–59

Mariners' Museum, Newport News, Virginia: 34–35

National Archives: 15, 18–19, 24T, 27, 48, 50T, 54T, 57

The George C. Neumann Collection, a gift of the Sun Company to Valley Forge National Historical Park, 1978, 67

U.S. Marine Corps, Washington D.C.: Front cover and 30 *Fighting Tops 29 May 1781*, by Charles Waterhouse, 16 *Landing at New Providence 3 March 1776*, by Charles Waterhouse, 23 *Launching of the Whitehaven Raid 22 April 1778*, by Charles Waterhouse, 39 Flag Raising at New Providence 28 January 1778 by Charles Waterhouse

U.S. Naval Academy Museum: 24–25, 32–33

U.S. Naval Historical Center, Washington, D.C.: Title page: 6–7, 10–11, 12T, 12–13, 17, 18, 22–23, 28–29, 62, 64–65

U.S. Government Printing Office: 14–15, 16T, 37 by Don Troiani, 54B

U.S. Senate Collection: 63

Robert W. Wilson, Woodruff, SC: 68

Maps by Jerry Malone